Mastering Git and GitHub: Version Control for Every Developer

A Complete Guide to Collaborating with Git and Managing Code Repositories

BOOZMAN RICHARD

BOOKER BLUNT

Table of Content

TABLE OF CONTENTS

INTRODUCTION

MASTERING GIT AND GITHUB: VERSION CONTROL FOR EVERY DEVELOPER

In the world of modern software development, **version control** has become an essential practice, with **Git** being the gold standard. Whether you are building a small application, contributing to an open-source project, or managing a large-scale enterprise software system, Git's distributed nature and powerful branching and merging capabilities have made it indispensable. But Git alone is not enough to manage complex development workflows — enter **GitHub**, the platform that takes Git's version control capabilities and enhances them with tools for collaboration, automation, and project management. Together, **Git and GitHub** empower developers to not only track and manage code changes but also to work more efficiently, streamline their workflows, and collaborate effectively with teams.

This book, **"Mastering Git and GitHub: Version Control for Every Developer,"** is designed to be a comprehensive guide for developers of all levels, from beginners to seasoned professionals, who want to master the fundamentals of Git and GitHub, as well as explore advanced features and workflows. Whether you're new to version control or looking to deepen your understanding of Git's powerful capabilities, this book offers you practical, real-world examples and step-by-step instructions to help you become proficient in both Git and GitHub.

Why Git and GitHub Matter

Version control is a crucial component of modern software development. It allows developers to track and manage changes to their codebase, making it easier to collaborate with teammates, review and merge contributions, and roll back changes when things go wrong. **Git**, the most popular distributed version control system (DVCS), offers unparalleled flexibility, speed, and efficiency when managing code.

On top of Git's robust functionality, **GitHub**—a web-based Git repository hosting service—adds layers of collaboration, continuous integration (CI), automation, and project management tools. GitHub transforms Git's raw version control into an environment where teams can work together seamlessly, where code review happens within the platform, and where DevOps tools like **GitHub Actions** help automate testing, deployment, and other critical workflows.

What You'll Learn in This Book

This book provides you with the knowledge and skills you need to fully utilize Git and GitHub in your daily development practices. Here's a brief overview of what's covered:

1. **Understanding Git and GitHub Fundamentals**: We begin by laying a strong foundation with Git's core concepts—repositories, commits, branches, and merges. From there, we introduce GitHub and explore how it enhances Git with remote repositories, pull requests, and collaborative features.

2. **Basic and Advanced Git Operations**: From initializing a repository and making your first commit to more advanced topics like rebasing, stashing, and using Git hooks, we provide a comprehensive guide to all Git commands and workflows. Whether you need to track bugs, manage releases, or handle merge conflicts, we cover the practical tools and strategies you need.

3. **GitHub Features and Collaboration**: GitHub is more than just a place to store code. We dive deep into GitHub's collaborative tools like **pull requests**, **issues**, **wikis**, **discussions**, and **projects**. These features help you work together with other developers, track progress, and organize tasks effectively.

4. **Advanced GitHub Automation**: GitHub Actions is a powerful tool for automating your workflows. We explore

how to set up **CI/CD pipelines**, automate testing and deployment, and build a more efficient software delivery process directly within GitHub.

5. **Working with Git in Teams and Enterprises**: Git is a distributed system, but that doesn't mean working in teams is always straightforward. We discuss strategies for using Git in a team environment, handling large repositories, and managing security and access control in enterprise-grade projects.

6. **Real-World Case Studies and Best Practices**: Throughout the book, we provide real-world examples, case studies, and best practices to illustrate how Git and GitHub are used in popular open-source projects and large organizations. You'll learn from real-world scenarios and understand how Git and GitHub facilitate collaboration, maintain code quality, and scale with the demands of modern development.

7. **Mastering GitHub for Personal Projects**: We also focus on how GitHub can be a powerful tool for personal projects, including portfolios, blogs, and websites. Whether you're a solo developer looking to showcase your work or building a personal website using **GitHub Pages**, we provide step-by-step instructions to make the most of GitHub's hosting and version control capabilities.

8. **The Future of Git and GitHub**: As Git and GitHub continue to evolve, we discuss upcoming features, how

the landscape of version control is changing, and what the future holds for developers. We also explore alternative version control systems and trends like **GitOps**, helping you stay ahead in a constantly changing field.

Who This Book is For

This book is designed for developers of all experience levels. Whether you're a beginner just starting to learn Git or an experienced developer looking to explore advanced GitHub features, this book offers something for everyone. By the end of this book, you will:

- Master Git's command-line operations and workflows.
- Leverage GitHub's collaboration and automation features to streamline your development process.
- Understand how to use Git and GitHub effectively in both personal and team-based projects.
- Stay current with the latest Git and GitHub features and workflows.

If you're looking to **advance your software development skills, boost your team's collaboration**, or **streamline your deployment process**, this book will provide you with the tools and knowledge you need to succeed.

A Practical Approach to Learning

This book focuses on providing **practical, hands-on knowledge** that you can apply to your real-world development projects. Every concept is illustrated with **step-by-step examples** and **practical exercises** designed to help you quickly understand and implement Git and GitHub in your own workflow. You'll not only learn how to use these tools but also why they are effective and how they can help you and your team improve the development process.

Whether you're looking to improve your individual workflow, manage large teams, or automate your CI/CD pipeline, **"Mastering Git and GitHub: Version Control for Every Developer"** equips you with the essential skills to leverage Git and GitHub in all areas of software development. Let's embark on this journey to master the tools that have transformed the world of version control and collaboration.

CHAPTER 1

INTRODUCTION TO GIT AND GITHUB

What is Version Control and Why is it Important?

Version control is a system that allows developers to track and manage changes to code over time. It is a critical tool in the development process because it enables collaboration, ensures code integrity, and maintains a history of code modifications. Without version control, developers would face difficulties in managing different versions of their code, especially in a team environment. Here are the primary benefits:

1. **Collaboration:** Multiple developers can work on the same project simultaneously without overwriting each other's changes.
2. **History Tracking:** Every change made to the code is recorded, allowing developers to revert to previous versions if something breaks.
3. **Conflict Resolution:** Version control makes it easier to merge changes from different contributors, highlighting conflicts that need to be resolved.

4. **Backup:** In case of a system failure, having a version-controlled repository means you always have a backup of your code.

Without version control, developers would have to manually manage versions, potentially leading to inconsistent results, loss of work, and difficulty in debugging. By using version control, you ensure that changes are systematic and that each modification is documented and traceable.

The History of Git and GitHub

- **Git:** Git was created in 2005 by Linus Torvalds, the same person who created the Linux operating system. The initial purpose was to manage the source code of Linux, which was growing rapidly in complexity and required a more efficient version control system. Git was designed to be fast, distributed, and flexible, unlike the centralized version control systems that were commonly used at the time. Its decentralized nature allows developers to work offline, and it can handle large codebases effectively.

- **GitHub:** GitHub was founded in 2008 by Tom Preston-Werner, Chris Wanstrath, PJ Hyett, and Scott Chacon. It was created to provide a cloud-based platform where developers could host and share their Git repositories. GitHub integrates Git's functionality with a user-friendly interface, social features like forks, pull requests, and a

13

wiki, making it the go-to platform for code collaboration and open-source projects. It quickly gained popularity due to its simplicity and community-driven model.

Together, Git and GitHub have become the de facto standard for version control and collaboration in software development.

Difference Between Git and GitHub

While Git and GitHub are often used together, they serve different purposes:

- **Git** is a **version control system**. It is a tool that runs on your local machine and allows you to track changes to files, manage different versions of a project, and collaborate with others by merging changes. Git works entirely offline and can be used independently of any web-based platforms.
- **GitHub** is a **hosting service** for Git repositories. It provides a cloud-based platform where you can store, manage, and collaborate on Git repositories. GitHub extends Git by adding a web interface, issue tracking, pull requests, wikis, and more. While Git is the underlying version control tool, GitHub is a platform that makes it easier to collaborate and share code.

In short, **Git** is the tool that tracks and manages your project history, and **GitHub** is the platform that hosts and collaborates on your Git repositories.

Basic Concepts of Version Control: Commits, Branches, and Repositories

- **Commits:** A commit in Git represents a snapshot of your project at a particular point in time. Each commit contains the changes you made, who made the changes, and a commit message that describes the purpose of the change. Commits create a history of your project, allowing you to track what was changed and why.

- **Branches:** A branch is a separate line of development. In Git, the default branch is typically called "master" (or "main" in newer versions). You can create new branches to work on different features or bug fixes without affecting the main project. Once the work on a branch is complete, it can be merged back into the main branch.

- **Repositories:** A repository (or "repo") is a collection of files and their change history. In Git, a repository tracks the entire history of a project, including every commit and branch. Repositories can be local (on your machine) or remote (on a server like GitHub).

Why Every Developer Should Use Git and GitHub

1. **Efficient Collaboration:** Git allows developers to work simultaneously on the same project without conflicts. GitHub makes it easy to share your code and contribute to others' projects by using features like forks and pull requests.

2. **Backup and Recovery:** With Git, your entire project history is stored in the repository. Even if you make a mistake, you can always go back to a previous version of the code, preventing data loss.

3. **Code Integrity:** Using Git ensures that no one can make changes to the code without it being tracked. This prevents errors from slipping through undetected and ensures that all changes are reviewed and properly integrated.

4. **Version History and Traceability:** Git and GitHub provide a full history of changes, making it easy to trace the origin of bugs and other issues. This history also serves as documentation, helping you understand why changes were made.

5. **Open Source Contribution:** GitHub is home to millions of open-source projects. As a developer, using Git and GitHub makes it easy to contribute to open-source communities and collaborate on shared codebases.

6. **CI/CD Integration:** GitHub integrates with Continuous Integration (CI) and Continuous Deployment (CD) tools,

making it easier to automate the build, testing, and deployment processes.

In short, Git and GitHub help developers work more efficiently, collaborate with others, and maintain high-quality, well-documented code.

Setting Up Git and GitHub

Here's how you can set up Git and GitHub on your local machine:

1. **Install Git:**
   o On **Windows**, you can download and install Git from git-scm.com. Follow the installation instructions, which are mostly defaults.
   o On **macOS**, Git is usually pre-installed. You can check by typing `git --version` in the terminal. If it's not installed, you can install it via Homebrew with the command: `brew install git`.
   o On **Linux**, you can install Git using the package manager for your distribution. For example, on Ubuntu, you can use: `sudo apt install git`.
2. **Configure Git:** After installing Git, you need to configure your username and email address. This is essential because Git uses this information to associate commits with your identity.

17

```
arduino
```

```
git config --global user.name "Your Name"
git     config     --global     user.email
"your.email@example.com"
```

3. **Create a GitHub Account:** Go to github.com and create a free account. Once you've signed up, you can create repositories, contribute to projects, and use all the features that GitHub offers.

4. **Set Up SSH for Secure Authentication:** To securely interact with GitHub, you can generate an SSH key pair and add it to your GitHub account. This will allow you to clone, pull, and push to repositories without needing to enter your password each time. GitHub has detailed instructions on how to do this.

5. **Create Your First Repository on GitHub:**
   o Go to GitHub, click on the "New" button to create a new repository.
   o Give it a name and decide if you want it to be public or private.
   o Once created, you can clone this repository to your local machine:

   ```bash
   bash
   ```

```
git                            clone
https://github.com/yourusername/you
r-repository.git
```

6. **Start Working with Git:** Now you're ready to start using Git locally. You can make changes, commit them, and push them back to GitHub.

This chapter sets the stage for everything that follows by introducing the fundamental concepts of version control, Git, and GitHub. It explains why these tools are essential for every developer and walks through setting up Git and GitHub to get you started on your coding journey.

4o mini

You said:

Chapter 2: Getting Started with Git • Installing Git on different operating systems. • Configuring Git (username, email, and default editor). • Understanding the Git command line interface. • The basic Git workflow: clone, add, commit, push, pull.

ChatGPT said:

Chapter 2: Getting Started with Git

Installing Git on Different Operating Systems

Git is a cross-platform tool, meaning it can be installed on various operating systems, including Windows, macOS, and Linux. Below are the instructions for installing Git on each:

Windows:

1. **Download Git**:
   - Go to the official Git website at https://git-scm.com/download/win and the download will start automatically.
   - Choose the version that matches your system architecture (32-bit or 64-bit).
2. **Run the Installer**:
   - After downloading, run the installer. Follow the default settings during the installation process unless you have specific needs. Here are some important steps to consider during installation:
     - **Choosing the default editor**: During installation, you'll be asked to select a text editor. If you're unsure, the default is usually Vim, but you can choose others like Notepad++ or Visual Studio Code.
     - **Adjusting your PATH environment**: Select "Use Git from the command line

and also from 3rd-party software" to ensure Git is available in the terminal.

3. **Finish the Installation**:

   o Complete the installation by clicking "Finish". You can now use Git from the command prompt or PowerShell.

macOS:

1. **Using Homebrew**:

   o If you have Homebrew installed, you can simply run the following command in the terminal:

   ```
   nginx
   ```

   ```
   brew install git
   ```

2. **Manual Installation**:

   o Alternatively, you can download the Git installer for macOS from https://git-scm.com/download/mac and follow the installation steps.

3. **Verify Installation**:

   o Once installed, open the Terminal and type:

   ```
   css
   ```

   ```
   git --version
   ```

21

o   If Git is correctly installed, it will display the version number.

Linux:

Git is generally available through the package manager of most Linux distributions. Here are the commands for some common distros:

- **Ubuntu/Debian**:

```sql
sudo apt update
sudo apt install git
```

- **Fedora**:

```nginx
sudo dnf install git
```

- **CentOS**:

```nginx
sudo yum install git
```

Once installed, you can verify the installation with:

```
css
```

```
git --version
```

Configuring Git (Username, Email, and Default Editor)

Once Git is installed, you need to configure it with your identity and preferred text editor. This information will be attached to your commits, ensuring they are associated with the correct person and context.

Configuring Username and Email:

Git uses your name and email address to associate commits with you. To configure these settings, use the following commands in the terminal:

- Set your username:

```
arduino
```

```
git config --global user.name "Your Name"
```

- Set your email:

```
nginx
```

```
git config --global user.email "your.email@example.com"
```

The `--global` flag ensures that these settings apply to all repositories on your system. If you want to use a different name or email for a specific repository, you can configure them locally by omitting the `--global` flag when running the commands inside that repository.

Setting the Default Editor:

Git needs an editor for writing commit messages. By default, it may use a command-line editor like Vim. However, you can choose a text editor you're more comfortable with.

For **Visual Studio Code** (VS Code), use:

```css
git config --global core.editor "code --wait"
```

For **Sublime Text**, use:

```arduino
git config --global core.editor "subl -n -w"
```

For **Atom**, use:

```arduino
git config --global core.editor "atom --wait"
```

If you prefer **Vim**, you don't need to make any changes, as it's the default editor. You can also choose from many other text editors like Emacs, Nano, or Notepad++.

Understanding the Git Command Line Interface

Git's command-line interface (CLI) is where you'll execute most Git operations. Here's an overview of the key commands:

- **git init**: Initializes a new Git repository in your current directory.
- **git clone [url]**: Clones a remote repository to your local machine.
- **git status**: Shows the status of the repository, including changes that have been staged, modified, or untracked.
- **git add [file]**: Stages changes to be committed. You can add individual files or use `git add .` to stage all modified files.
- **git commit -m "message"**: Commits the staged changes with a descriptive message.
- **git push [remote] [branch]**: Pushes your local commits to a remote repository (e.g., GitHub).
- **git pull [remote] [branch]**: Pulls the latest changes from a remote repository to your local branch.
- **git log**: Displays the commit history of the repository.

The Git CLI is very powerful and versatile, allowing you to perform a wide range of actions to manage your code. Over time, you'll get comfortable with common commands and workflows.

The Basic Git Workflow: Clone, Add, Commit, Push, Pull

Git follows a simple workflow for tracking and managing changes. Here's how the basic process works:

1. **Clone**:
   o When you start working on an existing repository, you need to clone it to your local machine. This copies all the code and version history from the remote repository (e.g., GitHub) to your computer.

   ```bash
   git                              clone
   https://github.com/username/reposit
   ory.git
   ```

   o After cloning, you have a local of the project, and you can start making changes.
2. **Add**:
   o After modifying files, Git needs to know what changes you want to track. You use `git add` to stage the changes.

26

```
csharp
```

```
git add filename
```

- ○ You can also stage all modified files at once:

```
csharp
```

```
git add .
```

- ○ This command adds changes to the "staging area" in preparation for a commit.

3. **Commit**:
   - ○ Once you've staged your changes, you commit them to your local repository. The commit captures the state of your code at that moment.

```
sql
```

```
git commit -m "Your commit message"
```

   - ○ The commit message should be descriptive, explaining what changes were made.

4. **Push**:
   - ○ After committing your changes, you push them to the remote repository (e.g., GitHub) so others can see and collaborate on them.

```
css
```

27

```
git push origin main
```

- o This sends your local commits to the remote repository, updating it with your changes.

5. **Pull**:

- o Before pushing your changes, you should always make sure your local repository is up to date with the remote repository. Use `git pull` to fetch and merge the latest changes.

```
css
```

```
git pull origin main
```

- o This ensures you're working with the most recent version of the code, avoiding conflicts with changes made by others.

By following this basic workflow—**clone, add, commit, push, pull**—you can keep track of your code, collaborate with others, and maintain an organized development process. This is the foundation for all version control with Git, and you'll build upon it as you learn more advanced concepts.

This chapter has equipped you with the basics of setting up Git, configuring it for your needs, and using the essential commands to get started with version control. The next chapters will delve deeper into more advanced Git features, branching strategies, and collaboration workflows.

CHAPTER 3

GIT FUNDAMENTALS: UNDERSTANDING GIT REPOSITORIES

What are Git Repositories?

A **Git repository** (or "repo") is a storage space where your project's files and their version history are kept. It contains all the files in your project, as well as a history of changes made to those files. Git uses this repository to track every modification to every file in the project, enabling version control. There are two types of repositories: **local** and **remote**.

The repository records every commit, which is a snapshot of your project at a given point in time. With each commit, you are effectively capturing a record of your work, making it easy to track changes, collaborate with others, and revert to previous states if necessary.

A Git repository consists of:

- **Working Directory**: The files that are currently being worked on.

- **Staging Area**: A space where changes are prepared before being committed.
- **Commit History**: A log of all commits that provides the history of changes made to the repository.
- **Branches**: A separate line of development within the repository.

Local vs. Remote Repositories

- **Local Repository:** A **local repository** is stored on your local machine. It is a private of the repository where you can make changes, commit those changes, and review the history of your project. The local repository consists of the working directory, staging area, and the `.git` directory where all the versioning information is stored.
  - **Advantages**:
    - You can work offline.
    - Local repositories are fast because they don't require internet access.
    - All Git commands can be executed locally (e.g., `git status`, `git add`, `git commit`).
- **Remote Repository:** A **remote repository** is hosted on a server (e.g., GitHub, GitLab, Bitbucket) and is accessible over the internet. It serves as a centralized location where you push and pull changes, enabling collaboration between developers.

31

- o **Advantages**:
  - Remote repositories allow teams to collaborate by sharing changes with others.
  - They provide backup for your code in case something happens to your local machine.
  - Remote repositories can be public (open-source projects) or private (for internal team collaboration).

A common workflow involves creating a local repository on your computer and then pushing changes to a remote repository, so others can access and collaborate on the project.

Creating a New Repository and Cloning an Existing One

Creating a New Repository:

To create a new Git repository, you can either create an empty repository or initialize one with an existing project.

1. **Create a New Repository Locally**: Navigate to your project folder and run the following command:

```csharp

git init
```

This command initializes a new Git repository in the current directory. It creates a `.git` directory that contains all the information needed to track versions and manage the repository.

2. **Create a New Repository on GitHub (Remote Repository)**:
   - First, log into your GitHub account and create a new repository on the GitHub website.
   - Then, to link the remote repository to your local machine, use the following commands:

   ```csharp
   git remote add origin https://github.com/yourusername/your-repository.git
   ```

   - Finally, you can push your code to GitHub with:

   ```css
   git push -u origin main
   ```

Cloning an Existing Repository:

If you want to work on an existing project, you can **clone** a repository from GitHub (or another Git host) to your local machine. This command copies the entire history and contents of the remote repository, making it available locally:

1. **Clone a Repository from GitHub**:

```bash
git                                          clone
https://github.com/username/repository.gi
t
```

This will create a new folder named `repository` (or any name you specify) and all files, branches, and commit history to that directory.

2. **Clone a Specific Branch**: If you want to clone a specific branch from the remote repository, use:

```bash
git        clone        -b        branch-name
https://github.com/username/repository.gi
t
```

The .git Directory

The `.git` directory is where Git stores all the metadata and history for your project. It is located in the root of your repository and contains several subdirectories and files that are vital for version control.

Some important components of the `.git` directory include:

- **objects**: Stores all the data related to your repository, including the files and history of every commit.
- **refs**: Contains references to the different branches and tags in your repository.
- **config**: Stores configuration settings for your repository, such as remotes and user settings.
- **HEAD**: A file that points to the current branch you are working on.

The `.git` directory is critical for the functioning of Git, and you should never edit or delete it manually. It ensures that Git can track the project's history, branches, and changes.

Exploring the Structure of a Git Repository

A Git repository typically has the following structure:

1. **Working Directory**: This is the area where you do all your work. It consists of the actual files of your project that you are editing. When you modify files in this directory, they are considered **untracked** or **modified** until they are added to the staging area.
2. **Staging Area (Index)**: The staging area is where you prepare changes to be committed. When you run `git add`, you're adding changes to the staging area, which is like a holding zone before the changes are committed. The

staging area allows you to review and group changes before making them part of the project's history.

3. **Commit History**: After you commit the staged changes, they are recorded in the **commit history**. This is a record of all changes made to the project, stored in the Git repository. You can use `git log` to see the commit history, with details like commit IDs, authors, dates, and commit messages.

4. **Branches**: A Git repository can have multiple branches, allowing developers to work on different features or bug fixes in isolation. Each branch has its own commit history, and branches can be merged when the work is ready. The default branch is usually called `main` (formerly `master`).

5. **Remote Repositories**: If you are collaborating with others, your local repository will be linked to one or more **remote repositories** (like GitHub). A remote repository allows multiple developers to work on the same project and share changes via `git push` and `git pull`.

6. **Configuration Files**: Git repositories may also contain configuration files like `.gitignore` and `.gitattributes`. The `.gitignore` file tells Git which files to exclude from version control (e.g., build files, sensitive data, etc.). The `.gitattributes` file defines attributes for paths, such as line endings and merge strategies.

This chapter has introduced the concept of Git repositories, explaining their purpose and key components. It covered the differences between local and remote repositories, as well as how to create and clone repositories. Additionally, we explored the .git directory and its essential role in Git's functionality. In the next chapters, we'll dive deeper into advanced Git features, including branching and merging, and how to effectively manage your repositories for team collaboration.

CHAPTER 4

BASIC GIT COMMANDS AND WORKFLOW

Git is designed to simplify the version control process with a series of commands that allow developers to track changes, collaborate with others, and manage different versions of their code. In this chapter, we'll go through some of the fundamental Git commands and the typical workflow you'll use when interacting with a Git repository. These commands form the foundation of how Git works, enabling you to perform the essential tasks of version control.

Understanding `git init,` `git` `clone,` `git` `status,` *and* `git` `add`

1. `git init` – Initializing a New Git Repository

- **Purpose**: `git init` initializes a new Git repository in the current directory.
- **Usage**: This command is used when you want to start version controlling a project from scratch. It creates a new `.git` directory that stores all the version control information.

Example:

38

```
bash

git init
```

This command is often used at the start of a project or when you want to make an existing folder a Git repository. After running `git init`, the directory becomes a Git repository, and you can start tracking files and committing changes.

2. `git clone` – Cloning a Remote Repository

- **Purpose**: `git clone` copies a repository from a remote location (like GitHub) to your local machine, including the full project history.
- **Usage**: This command is used to download an entire repository and its history from a remote server to your local system. When you clone a repository, you also automatically set up a remote called `origin`, which is a reference to the original repository.

Example:

```
bash

git                                           clone
https://github.com/username/repository.gi
t
```

This will create a of the repository on your local machine, and you'll be able to interact with it as if it was your own. After cloning, you can start modifying files, committing changes, and pushing to or pulling from the remote repository.

3. `git status` – Checking the Current State

- **Purpose**: `git status` shows the current status of your working directory and staging area. It tells you what changes are staged for the next commit, what changes are not staged, and what files are untracked by Git.
- **Usage**: This command is helpful for checking which files need to be added to the staging area or which files have changes that are yet to be committed.

Example:

```bash
```

```
git status
```

You might see outputs like:

- o **Untracked files**: Files that Git is not tracking yet.
- o **Changes to be committed**: Files that are staged and ready to be committed.

o **Changes not staged for commit**: Files that have been modified but not staged yet.

4. `git add` – Staging Changes for Commit

- **Purpose**: `git add` is used to stage changes (modified or new files) for the next commit. When you modify a file, Git needs to know that you want to include these changes in your next commit.
- **Usage**: You can add specific files or all files in the current directory using this command.

Example:

```
bash
```

```
git add filename
git add .
```

o `git add filename`: Stages a specific file.
o `git add .`: Stages all changes in the current directory, including new, modified, or deleted files.

Once files are added to the staging area, they are prepared for a commit.

Working with Commits: `git commit`*, Commit Messages, and Commit History*

1. `git commit` – Recording Changes

- **Purpose**: `git commit` is used to record changes in the local repository after staging them with `git add`. Each commit creates a snapshot of the project at a specific point in time.
- **Usage**: It's important to write meaningful commit messages that describe the changes you made. A commit message should be concise and to the point, explaining *why* the change was made, not just *what* was changed.

Example:

```bash
```

```
git commit -m "Added feature to handle user
authentication"
```

The `-m` flag is used to provide the commit message directly from the command line. If you don't use `-m`, Git will open a text editor for you to type your message.

42

2. Commit Messages: Best Practices

Commit messages are crucial for keeping your Git history organized and making it easier to understand the reasoning behind changes. Here are some tips for writing good commit messages:

- Use the **imperative mood** (e.g., "Fix bug" instead of "Fixed bug").
- Keep the message under 50 characters for the subject line, with a more detailed explanation in the body if necessary.
- Explain why the change was made, not just what was changed.

3. `git log` – Viewing Commit History

- **Purpose**: `git log` shows the commit history of the repository, including each commit's ID (SHA-1 hash), author, date, and commit message.
- **Usage**: This command is useful for viewing the history of your repository and understanding what changes have been made over time.

Example:

```bash
git log
```

The output will look something like this:

```
sql
```

```
commit
9fceb02a4c0d4d1ab537d30c548ed7192482a5ac
Author: John Doe <johndoe@example.com>
Date:   Thu Apr 12 14:23:56 2025 -0400

    Added user authentication feature

commit
78b45e3f102cd2281c6b7e36c64de8ea85b50632
Author: John Doe <johndoe@example.com>
Date:   Wed Apr 11 09:11:32 2025 -0400

    Fixed bug with login page form
validation
```

You can use additional flags to customize the output, such as `git log --oneline` for a simplified view with just the commit IDs and messages.

Pushing and Pulling Changes: `git push` and `git pull`

1. `git push` – Sending Changes to a Remote Repository

- **Purpose**: `git push` is used to upload your commits to a remote repository, like GitHub. This makes your local changes available to others.

- **Usage**: When you push, you specify the remote repository (often named `origin`) and the branch you want to push to (usually `main`).

Example:

```bash
```

```
git push origin main
```

This pushes your local changes to the `main` branch of the `origin` remote repository.

2. `git pull` – Fetching Changes from a Remote Repository

- **Purpose**: `git pull` is used to fetch and integrate changes from a remote repository into your local branch. It is essentially a combination of `git fetch` (which downloads changes) and `git merge` (which integrates the changes).
- **Usage**: Before pushing your changes, it's recommended to pull the latest changes from the remote repository to ensure you're working with the most up-to-date version of the code.

Example:

```bash
```

```
git pull origin main
```

This fetches changes from the `main` branch of the remote repository and merges them with your local `main` branch.

Working with the Staging Area

The **staging area** is where changes are prepared before they are committed. When you modify a file in your working directory, Git doesn't automatically track it. You have to explicitly add the file to the staging area using `git add`.

The staging area allows you to:

- Stage only specific changes you want to commit.
- Group changes together before committing them to maintain a clean project history.
- Check what is staged using `git status`.

You can unstage changes by using:

```bash
git reset <file>
```

This removes a file from the staging area but doesn't undo the changes made to the file.

Checking Out Previous Commits

Sometimes, you might want to revisit a previous commit. You can use `git checkout` to view or revert to a previous commit:

- **Viewing a Previous Commit:** To view a previous commit, use the following command with the commit hash:

  bash

  ```
  git checkout <commit-id>
  ```

- **Creating a New Branch from a Previous Commit:** If you want to create a new branch based on an older commit, use:

  bash

  ```
  git checkout -b new-branch <commit-id>
  ```

- **Reverting to a Previous Commit:** You can also revert your repository to a previous commit, effectively undoing changes made after that commit:

  bash

  ```
  git revert <commit-id>
  ```

By using these commands, you can navigate through the history of your project, retrieve old versions of files, and make changes based on earlier states of the repository.

In this chapter, we've covered the essential Git commands that every developer should master. You learned how to initialize and clone repositories, check the status of your project, add changes to the staging area, make commits, and interact with remote repositories using `git push` and `git pull`. Additionally, we explored how to work with the staging area and checkout previous commits to navigate your project's history effectively. These core skills will be essential as you continue working with Git in both solo and collaborative projects.

CHAPTER 5

BRANCHING AND MERGING IN GIT

Branching and merging are core concepts in Git that allow you to develop features, fix bugs, or experiment with new ideas in isolation, without affecting the main codebase. This chapter explores these key concepts in Git, how to manage them effectively, and best practices to follow when working with branches.

What is Branching in Git and Why is it Important?

A **branch** in Git is essentially a pointer to a specific commit in the repository. Git branches allow you to create parallel development paths, making it possible to work on new features or fix bugs without interfering with the main codebase. The default branch in a Git repository is typically called `main` (or `master`), and all new branches are typically created from this branch.

Why is branching important?

1. **Isolation of Changes**: Branching allows you to isolate different tasks or features. For example, you can work on

49

a new feature in one branch while keeping the main branch stable.

2. **Parallel Development**: Multiple developers can work on different branches at the same time. Each developer can work on separate features or fixes, and when they're done, the changes can be merged back into the main branch.

3. **Risk Mitigation**: Branches let you experiment with new ideas without fear of breaking the main codebase. If the experiment doesn't work out, you can discard the branch without affecting the stable version of the project.

4. **Cleaner History**: Using branches to separate different tasks makes it easier to manage your Git history. Instead of having a history of commits mixed with unrelated changes, you have isolated branches that represent distinct features or fixes.

Creating and Switching Branches: `git branch` *and* `git checkout`

Creating a New Branch

To create a new branch, you use the `git branch` command. This command creates a new branch, but it doesn't automatically switch you to that branch.

Example:

`bash`

```
git branch new-feature
```

This creates a new branch called `new-feature`. However, you are still on the current branch (typically `main`).

Switching to a Branch

To switch to the newly created branch (or any existing branch), you use the `git checkout` command:

Example:

```
bash
```

```
git checkout new-feature
```

This command moves you from your current branch (e.g., `main`) to the `new-feature` branch, allowing you to start working on it.

Alternatively, you can use a combined command to create and switch to a branch in one step:

```
bash
```

```
git checkout -b new-feature
```

This command does two things:

1. Creates the `new-feature` branch.

2. Switches to the `new-feature` branch.

Listing Branches

To see a list of all branches in your repository, use:

```bash
bash
```

```bash
git branch
```

The current branch will be highlighted with an asterisk *.

Merging Branches: `git merge` and Handling Merge Conflicts

Once you've made changes in a branch and are ready to bring them back into the main codebase, you need to **merge** the branch. Merging is the process of taking changes from one branch and applying them to another.

Merging a Branch with `git merge`

To merge a branch into your current branch, first ensure that you're on the branch you want to merge into (typically `main` or `master`), and then run:

Example:

```bash
bash
```

```
git checkout main  # Switch to the main branch
git merge new-feature   # Merge the new-feature
branch into main
```

This command will combine the changes from the new-feature branch into the main branch. If there are no conflicts, the merge will be automatic and Git will create a new commit that represents the merged changes.

Handling Merge Conflicts

Merge conflicts occur when Git is unable to automatically merge two sets of changes. This usually happens when two branches modify the same lines in the same file, or when one branch deletes a file that the other branch modifies.

When a merge conflict happens, Git will stop and mark the conflicting areas in the affected files. You will see something like this in the conflicted files:

```bash
<<<<<<< HEAD
// Changes from the current branch (main)
=======
 // Changes from the branch you're merging (new-
feature)
>>>>>>> new-feature
```

You need to manually resolve the conflict by choosing one version of the changes, combining both, or making other adjustments. After resolving the conflict, stage the changes using `git add`, and then complete the merge with a commit:

```bash
git add <file>
git commit
```

Abort a Merge

If you decide that the merge is not what you wanted, you can abort it using:

```bash
git merge --abort
```

This will return you to the state before the merge began, allowing you to try again or make alternative decisions.

Fast-Forward and Recursive Merges

Git has different types of merge strategies depending on the circumstances. The two most common merge strategies are **fast-forward** and **recursive**.

Fast-Forward Merge

A **fast-forward merge** occurs when the current branch is directly behind the branch being merged. In other words, the commits from the merged branch can be added directly on top of the current branch without any divergent history.

Example:

- If the `main` branch has not diverged and the `new-feature` branch only adds commits after `main`, Git can simply fast-forward the `main` branch to include the commits from `new-feature`.

To perform a fast-forward merge, you don't need any special flags, and the process is automatic when you run `git merge`.

Recursive Merge

A **recursive merge** happens when the branches have diverged, meaning they have different commits that need to be reconciled. Git will create a new commit that merges the changes from both branches into one.

Example:

- If `main` has a commit that `new-feature` doesn't have, and `new-feature` has a commit that `main` doesn't have,

Git will automatically create a merge commit to combine the two.

Git will use the **recursive strategy** when necessary to merge the branches, and it may require you to resolve conflicts manually if changes overlap.

Best Practices for Branching and Merging

Branching and merging can quickly become confusing if not handled properly. Below are some best practices to keep your branches and merges organized:

1. **Use Descriptive Branch Names**:
    o Name your branches based on the feature or task you are working on, e.g., `feature/login-system`, `bugfix/fix-header`, or `chore/update-dependencies`.

2. **Work in Small, Focused Branches**:
    o Avoid making large, sweeping changes on a single branch. Instead, create a new branch for each feature or bug fix. This makes it easier to manage changes and reduces the likelihood of conflicts.

3. **Keep Branches Short-Lived**:
    o Try to avoid keeping branches open for too long. Regularly merge them back into the main branch

(or another target branch) to keep the codebase up-to-date. Long-lived branches are more likely to result in complex merges.

4. **Pull and Merge Regularly**:
   - Frequently pull the latest changes from the main branch into your feature branch to keep it up-to-date. This reduces the chances of running into large merge conflicts later on.
   - Example: Before merging a feature branch into the main branch, ensure the feature branch is up-to-date:

   bash

   ```
   git pull origin main
   ```

5. **Use Pull Requests (for Collaborative Projects)**:
   - In team settings, use **Pull Requests (PRs)** to review and discuss changes before they are merged. This helps ensure the quality of the code and allows team members to provide feedback.

6. **Merge Regularly, Avoid Rewriting History**:
   - When merging, avoid using `git rebase` on shared branches because it rewrites history. Instead, use `git merge` to maintain a clear history of all changes. Merging preserves the

history and shows when and why changes were made.

7. **Avoid Merging Unfinished Features**:

   o Always ensure your branch is complete and tested before merging. If your feature is not ready, don't merge it into the main branch. Use **feature flags** or **work-in-progress branches** for unfinished work.

In this chapter, we've covered the essential concepts of **branching** and **merging** in Git. You learned how to create and switch branches, how merging works, and how to resolve conflicts when they arise. We also explored fast-forward and recursive merges and provided best practices for working with branches effectively. Mastering these concepts will help you maintain a clean and efficient workflow, whether you're working solo or collaborating in a team.

CHAPTER 6

GITHUB BASICS: UNDERSTANDING REPOSITORIES AND COLLABORATION

GitHub is one of the most popular platforms for hosting Git repositories, collaborating on code, and contributing to open-source projects. This chapter will introduce you to the basics of GitHub, explain how it differs from Git, and guide you through creating repositories, understanding GitHub's interface, and making your first commit.

What is GitHub and How is It Different from Git?

While Git is a version control system that runs locally on your computer to track changes to files, **GitHub** is a web-based platform that hosts Git repositories and adds additional features for collaboration and project management.

Key Differences:

1. **Git**:

o A version control tool used to track changes in files and manage different versions of a project.

o Works entirely on your local machine, allowing you to commit, branch, and merge changes locally.

2. **GitHub**:

o A cloud-based service that stores Git repositories remotely, allowing for collaboration among developers worldwide.

o Provides additional tools like issue tracking, pull requests, wikis, and GitHub Actions to facilitate team collaboration, continuous integration, and more.

o Integrates with other services like CI/CD tools and issue trackers, and offers social features such as forking, starring, and following projects.

In short, **Git** is the tool you use to track versions of your code, and **GitHub** is the platform where you can store your code remotely and collaborate with others. GitHub makes it easier to share your work, track issues, and manage the development of software projects.

Creating a GitHub Account and Setting Up Repositories

To begin using GitHub, you'll first need to create an account and set up a repository where you can store and collaborate on your code.

Creating a GitHub Account

1. Go to GitHub.com and click on the "Sign up" button.
2. Fill in your username, email address, and password.
3. Verify your email address by following the instructions in the confirmation email sent to you.
4. Complete any necessary setup steps to configure your account (e.g., selecting a plan, customizing your profile).

Setting Up a New Repository

1. **Create a New Repository**:
   o After logging into GitHub, click on the "New" button (usually on your profile page or in the repositories section).
   o You'll be prompted to enter a name for your repository (e.g., `my-first-repo`).
   o Add an optional description of the project.
   o Choose whether the repository will be **public** or **private** (public repositories are visible to

everyone, while private ones are only accessible by collaborators you invite).

o   Initialize the repository with a README file (optional but recommended) so that others can understand the project.

2.   **Clone the Repository to Your Local Machine**:

o   Once the repository is created, GitHub will show you a URL (HTTPS or SSH) to clone the repository to your local machine.

o   Use the following command to clone the repository:

```
bash
```

```
git                          clone
https://github.com/yourusername/you
r-repository.git
```

o   This command copies the repository to your local machine, allowing you to work with it locally.

Understanding GitHub's Interface: Issues, Pull Requests, and Actions

GitHub has a rich interface that includes various features for collaboration, issue tracking, and automation. Let's go through some of the key components of GitHub's interface:

1. Issues

- **What are Issues?**: Issues in GitHub are used to track bugs, enhancements, tasks, or any other project-related discussions. They are useful for keeping track of work that needs to be done or problems that need fixing.
- **How to Create an Issue**:
    1. Go to the "Issues" tab in your repository.
    2. Click the "New issue" button.
    3. Provide a title and description of the issue, and choose labels (e.g., bug, enhancement) to categorize it.
    4. Click "Submit new issue."
- **Why Issues are Important**: Issues help you and your collaborators organize and manage work efficiently. They allow you to track ongoing work and ensure that important tasks are completed on time.

2. Pull Requests

- **What is a Pull Request (PR)?**: A pull request is a request to merge changes from one branch into another, typically from a feature branch into the main branch. It allows you to propose changes and have them reviewed before they are merged.
- **How to Create a Pull Request**:

1. After pushing your changes to a feature branch on GitHub, go to the "Pull requests" tab.

2. Click the "New pull request" button.

3. Choose the base branch (usually `main`) and compare it with the branch containing your changes.

4. Add a title and description to explain the changes.

5. Click "Create pull request."

- **Why Pull Requests are Important**: Pull requests are essential for collaborative development. They enable team members to review code, discuss proposed changes, and catch potential issues before they are merged into the main codebase.

3. GitHub Actions

- **What are GitHub Actions?**: GitHub Actions is an automation tool that allows you to create workflows for continuous integration (CI), continuous deployment (CD), and other tasks. Actions automate various processes, such as running tests, building projects, or deploying code.

- **How to Use GitHub Actions**:
  1. In your repository, go to the "Actions" tab.
  2. You can either use a pre-configured template or create your own custom workflow.

3. Workflows are defined in YAML files and can be triggered by events like pushes, pull requests, or issue comments.

4. GitHub Actions will execute the specified tasks automatically when the event occurs.

- **Why GitHub Actions are Important**: GitHub Actions streamline development workflows, automate testing, and help maintain code quality by running checks and deployments automatically.

Making Your First Commit on GitHub

Once you have your repository set up and cloned, you're ready to start making changes and committing them. A commit represents a snapshot of your project at a specific point in time.

Making Changes Locally:

1. Navigate to the cloned repository on your local machine.

2. Open or create files that you want to change.

3. After making changes, you need to stage the files using:

```bash
git add .
```

This stages all changes, preparing them for commit.

Committing Changes:

1. Once your changes are staged, commit them to your local repository:

   bash

   ```
   git commit -m "Initial commit with project
   setup"
   ```

2. This commit includes a message that describes the changes you made. Good commit messages help other developers understand the purpose of the commit.

Pushing to GitHub:

To share your changes on GitHub, push your commits to the remote repository:

bash

```
git push origin main
```

- `origin` refers to the remote repository (GitHub in this case).
- `main` is the branch you are pushing to (typically the default branch).

66

Now, your local changes will appear on GitHub. You can go to your GitHub repository and see the commit reflected in the "Commits" tab.

In this chapter, we introduced you to the basics of GitHub, including its purpose, how to create and set up repositories, and how to work with GitHub's interface. You also learned about key features like Issues, Pull Requests, and Actions, which are vital for collaboration. Finally, you made your first commit on GitHub and pushed changes to the remote repository, marking the beginning of your journey with GitHub. As you continue to use GitHub, you'll dive deeper into these features and explore how they enhance your development workflow.

CHAPTER 7

COLLABORATING WITH OTHERS USING GITHUB

GitHub is not just a platform for storing code; it is a powerful tool for collaboration. It enables developers from all over the world to work together, review code, and contribute to projects efficiently. In this chapter, we will dive into how you can collaborate with others on GitHub by cloning, forking repositories, managing pull requests, and following best practices for team-based development.

Cloning and Forking Repositories

When working with others on GitHub, you often need to either clone a repository (if you're working on the same project) or fork it (if you're contributing to someone else's project). These two actions are essential for collaborating with others.

1. Cloning a Repository

Cloning a repository means making a of an entire repository (including its history) from GitHub to your local machine. It is the first step if you want to start working on a project stored on GitHub.

68

- **How to Clone a Repository**:
    1. Go to the GitHub repository page.
    2. Click the **"Code"** button, then the URL (either HTTPS or SSH).
    3. In your terminal, navigate to the directory where you want the project to be stored.
    4. Run the `git clone` command with the copied URL:

    ```bash
    git                                clone
    https://github.com/username/reposit
    ory.git
    ```

This will create a local of the repository, allowing you to work on it locally and push changes back to GitHub.

2. Forking a Repository

Forking is the process of creating a of someone else's repository under your GitHub account. This is commonly used when you want to contribute to an open-source project but don't have write access to the original repository. Forking allows you to experiment freely without affecting the original project.

- **How to Fork a Repository**:
    1. Go to the GitHub repository you want to fork.

2. Click the **"Fork"** button (usually at the top right of the repository page).

3. GitHub will create a of the repository under your own GitHub account, and you'll be redirected to your forked repository.

Once you've forked the repository, you can clone it to your local machine, make changes, and later submit a pull request to the original repository to propose your changes.

Pull Requests: What They Are and How They Work

A **pull request** (PR) is a request to merge changes from one branch (typically from a fork or a feature branch) into another branch (usually the main branch or another development branch). Pull requests allow others to review your changes, discuss them, and ensure the code is ready before merging it into the main project.

How to Create a Pull Request

1. After making changes to your forked repository or branch, push your changes to the remote repository.

2. Navigate to the repository on GitHub and switch to the branch containing your changes.

3. Click the **"Pull Request"** button (usually located next to the branch switcher).

70

4. Select the **base branch** (the branch you want to merge changes into, usually `main` or `master`), and the **compare branch** (the branch containing your changes).

5. Add a descriptive title and comment to explain the changes you're proposing, and then click **"Create Pull Request"**.

GitHub will show a summary of the changes between the base and compare branches. This allows the repository maintainers or other collaborators to review the differences before merging.

How Pull Requests Work:

- **Review**: Team members can review the pull request, discuss changes, and request modifications.
- **Approval**: Once the changes are reviewed and approved, the pull request can be merged into the base branch.
- **Merge**: The changes from the pull request are incorporated into the target branch.

Managing Pull Requests: Reviewing, Commenting, and Merging

Pull requests are a central feature for collaboration on GitHub, especially for open-source projects. As a collaborator or maintainer, you'll need to manage the pull requests submitted to your repositories. This includes reviewing the code, providing feedback, and merging changes when appropriate.

1. Reviewing Pull Requests

When you receive a pull request, you will want to review the proposed changes. GitHub provides several tools for reviewing pull requests:

- **Viewing Changes**: You can see what files have been changed, the differences between the files (using a side-by-side or unified diff view), and any specific line-by-line changes.
- **Reviewing the Code**: Look at the code, identify bugs, suggest improvements, and check for issues such as style inconsistencies, logic problems, or missing tests.
- **Inline Comments**: You can comment on specific lines of code within the pull request to suggest changes or ask questions. To add an inline comment, hover over the line of code you want to comment on and click the comment icon.

2. Commenting on Pull Requests

As a reviewer or contributor, you can comment on the entire pull request or specific lines of code. Comments are useful for:

- Asking questions about the code.
- Suggesting improvements or best practices.
- Highlighting issues or bugs.

To comment on a pull request:

1. Open the pull request.
2. Scroll down to the **"Conversation"** tab.
3. Add your comment in the text box at the bottom and click **"Comment"**.

You can also approve or request changes from the pull request:

- **Request Changes**: If you feel the pull request needs work before it's merged, you can request changes.
- **Approve**: Once you're satisfied with the changes, you can approve the pull request.

3. Merging Pull Requests

Once the pull request has been reviewed and all issues have been addressed, it is ready to be merged into the base branch.

- **How to Merge a Pull Request**:
    1. Go to the pull request page.
    2. Once everything is reviewed and approved, click the **"Merge Pull Request"** button.
    3. Choose the type of merge (usually **Create a merge commit** or **Squash and merge**), and add a commit message.
    4. Click **"Confirm Merge"**.

After merging, GitHub will update the base branch with the changes from the pull request.

- **Squash and Merge**: This option combines all the commits from the pull request into a single commit, making the commit history cleaner.
- **Rebase and Merge**: This option rebases the pull request on top of the base branch before merging it, which results in a linear history.
- **Create a Merge Commit**: This option keeps all the commits from the pull request in a merge commit, preserving the original commit history.

Once the pull request is merged, the branch can be safely deleted.

Best Practices for Collaboration on GitHub

Collaboration on GitHub requires good communication, discipline, and understanding of the workflow. To ensure a smooth collaboration process, follow these best practices:

1. **Use Clear Commit Messages**:
   - Commit messages should clearly describe the changes made. Avoid vague messages like "Fixed bug" or "Update file." Instead, use more descriptive messages such as "Fixed issue with login validation" or "Added user authentication feature."

74

2. **Branch for Every Feature or Bug Fix**:

   o Always create a separate branch for each new feature or bug fix. This keeps the project's history clean and allows you to work on different tasks without interfering with the main codebase.

3. **Keep Pull Requests Small and Focused**:

   o Aim to create pull requests that are small, focused, and easy to review. Large pull requests can be overwhelming to review and increase the chance of introducing bugs.

4. **Regularly Sync Your Branch with the Base Branch**:

   o Regularly pull changes from the main branch to your feature branch to stay up to date with the latest changes. This reduces the chances of merge conflicts when your pull request is ready to be merged.

5. **Be Responsive to Feedback**:

   o When reviewing pull requests or working on your own, be open to feedback. Address comments and suggestions promptly and make the necessary changes.

6. **Respect the Review Process**:

   o If you're a contributor, wait for your pull request to be reviewed before merging. If you're a reviewer, take the time to thoroughly check the code, ensure it follows coding standards, and test for bugs.

7. **Use Labels, Milestones, and Assignees**:
   - Use **labels** to categorize issues and pull requests (e.g., bug, enhancement, help wanted).
   - Assign tasks to team members using **assignees**.
   - Organize your work using **milestones** for major releases or features.

8. **Communicate Effectively**:
   - GitHub provides several tools for communication, such as pull request comments, issue comments, and discussions. Use these tools to ask questions, share feedback, and keep the team updated on progress.

In this chapter, we've explored how to collaborate effectively on GitHub. We discussed cloning and forking repositories, creating and managing pull requests, and best practices for code reviews and merging. Following these guidelines will help you work more efficiently with your team, keep the codebase organized, and ensure that the development process runs smoothly. As you gain more experience with GitHub, you'll become more comfortable with these tools and practices, enhancing your collaboration skills even further.

CHAPTER 8

ADVANCED GIT COMMANDS AND CONCEPTS

Git offers a variety of advanced commands and techniques that allow you to manage your project history more efficiently and handle complex scenarios. In this chapter, we'll dive into **cherry-picking, rebasing, squashing commits, resetting vs checking out**, and **stashing changes**. These concepts are essential for mastering Git and making your version control process more effective.

Cherry-Picking and Rebasing

1. Cherry-Picking:

Cherry-picking is the process of applying a specific commit from one branch to another, without merging the entire branch. This can be useful when you want to apply a fix or feature from a branch without including all the other changes in that branch.

- **Why Use Cherry-Picking?** Cherry-picking is useful when you need to bring in specific commits into a different branch without introducing the entire history of changes from the source branch. For example, if you have a bug fix on a feature branch that you want to apply to the `main` branch, but don't want to merge the entire feature branch, you can use cherry-picking.

- **How to Cherry-Pick a Commit**:
  1. Find the commit hash (SHA) you want to cherry-pick by using `git log`.
  2. Checkout the branch where you want to apply the commit.
  3. Run the `git cherry-pick` command with the commit hash:

  bash

  ```
  git cherry-pick <commit-hash>
  ```

  4. If the commit is applied successfully, Git will add it to your current branch as a new commit.
- **Handling Conflicts**: If there are conflicts during cherry-picking, Git will stop and ask you to resolve them. After resolving conflicts, stage the changes (`git add`) and complete the cherry-pick with:

  bash

  ```
  git cherry-pick --continue
  ```

2. Rebasing:

Rebasing is the process of reapplying commits from one branch onto another base branch. Unlike merging, which creates a merge commit, rebasing rewrites history to create a linear progression of commits.

- **Why Use Rebasing?** Rebasing is useful for maintaining a clean, linear history in your project. This is especially helpful when you want to avoid the clutter of merge commits and keep your project history easy to follow.
- **How to Rebase**:
    1. Checkout the branch you want to rebase.

       ```bash
       git checkout feature-branch
       ```

    2. Run the `git rebase` command to reapply the changes onto the target branch (e.g., `main`).

       ```bash
       git rebase main
       ```

    3. Git will reapply all the commits from `feature-branch` onto `main`. If there are no conflicts, the rebase will be automatic.
- **Handling Conflicts during Rebase**: If there are conflicts, Git will pause and ask you to resolve them. After resolving conflicts, you need to stage the changes (`git add`) and then continue the rebase:

```bash
git rebase --continue
```

- **Why Choose Rebase over Merge?**
  - **Merge** results in a commit history that may have multiple branches and merge commits, making the history more complex.
  - **Rebase** gives a linear history, which can make it easier to understand the changes over time. However, **rebase rewrites history**, so you should not rebase branches that have already been shared with others.

Squashing Commits

Squashing commits is the process of combining multiple commits into a single commit. This is particularly useful when you have made several small commits that represent a single logical change. Squashing commits helps keep the history cleaner and easier to understand.

- **Why Squash Commits?** Squashing commits is useful when you want to:
  - Clean up your commit history before merging a feature branch into `main`.
  - Avoid cluttering the history with minor commits that aren't meaningful on their own.

80

- **How to Squash Commits:** To squash commits, you can use **interactive rebase**:

    1. Start an interactive rebase with the command:

    ```bash
    git rebase -i HEAD~n
    ```

    Replace n with the number of commits you want to review (e.g., HEAD~3 for the last 3 commits).

    2. In the interactive rebase interface, change pick to squash (or s for short) for the commits you want to squash into the previous commit.

    3. After saving and closing the editor, Git will merge the commits and prompt you to write a commit message. You can combine the commit messages or provide a new one that summarizes the changes.

    4. Once the rebase is finished, your commits will be squashed into a single commit.

- **Example of Interactive Rebase:** Suppose you have the following commit history:

    ```sql
    pick a1b2c3 Commit 1
    pick d4e5f6 Commit 2
    ```

81

```
pick g7h8i9 Commit 3
```

After running `git rebase -i HEAD~3`, change it to:

```
sql
```

```
pick a1b2c3 Commit 1
squash d4e5f6 Commit 2
squash g7h8i9 Commit 3
```

This will squash Commit 2 and Commit 3 into Commit 1, resulting in a single commit.

git reset vs git checkout

Both `git reset` and `git checkout` are commands used to move around in Git history, but they work in different ways and serve different purposes.

1. git reset:

The `git reset` command is used to undo changes in your working directory and staging area. It can modify the commit history, which makes it a powerful but potentially dangerous tool.

- **Soft Reset (`git reset --soft`):**
    - o Moves the HEAD to a specific commit and leaves the changes in your staging area.

o   This allows you to modify the commit history without losing your changes.

Example:

```
bash
```

```
git reset --soft HEAD~1
```

- **Mixed Reset (default) (`git reset --mixed`):**
  - o   Moves the HEAD and un-stages the changes. The changes remain in your working directory but are no longer staged for commit.

Example:

```
bash
```

```
git reset HEAD~1
```

- **Hard Reset (`git reset --hard`):**
  - o   Resets the HEAD, staging area, and working directory to a specific commit. This discards all changes, so use it with caution.

Example:

```
bash
```

```
git reset --hard HEAD~1
```

2. git checkout:

The git checkout command is used to switch between branches or restore files in your working directory. Unlike git reset, git checkout doesn't modify the commit history.

- **Switching Branches**:

  bash

  ```
  git checkout feature-branch
  ```

- **Restoring Files**: You can use git checkout to restore files from a previous commit:

  bash

  ```
  git checkout HEAD~1 path/to/file
  ```

  This restores the file from the previous commit, without affecting other files in the working directory.

Stashing Changes with git stash

Stashing is a way to temporarily save changes that you don't want to commit yet. This is helpful when you're in the middle of working on something but need to switch contexts (e.g., switching to a different branch to address an urgent bug). You can stash your changes, switch branches, and come back to your stashed work later.

How to Use `git stash`:

- **Stashing Changes**: To save your uncommitted changes to a stash, run:

  bash

  ```
  git stash
  ```

- **Stashing with a Message**: You can add a message to the stash for better context:

  bash

  ```
  git stash save "Work in progress on feature X"
  ```

- **Listing Stashes**: To view all your stashes, use:

  bash

  ```
  git stash list
  ```

- **Applying Stashed Changes**: To apply the most recent stash, run:

  bash

85

```
git stash apply
```

If you want to apply a specific stash, use:

```
bash
```

```
git stash apply stash@{n}
```

- **Dropping Stashes**: Once you're done with a stash, you can remove it using:

```
bash
```

```
git stash drop stash@{n}
```

- **Pop the Stash**: If you want to apply the stash and remove it from the list, use:

```
bash
```

```
git stash pop
```

In this chapter, we covered several advanced Git commands and techniques that will help you manage your repository more efficiently. You learned how to **cherry-pick** specific commits, **rebase** for a cleaner commit history, **squash commits** for a more concise history, and how to use `git reset` vs. `git checkout` for different scenarios. Finally, we explored **stashing changes** to temporarily save work that you don't want to commit yet. Mastering these commands will give you more flexibility and control when working with Git.

CHAPTER 9

GITHUB ADVANCED FEATURES

GitHub offers powerful features that go beyond basic version control, enabling efficient project management, automated workflows, and even website hosting. In this chapter, we'll explore advanced features of GitHub that help with **issue management**, **GitHub Pages for website creation**, **using GitHub Actions for Continuous Integration (CI)**, and **writing and using GitHub workflows** to automate tasks.

Managing Issues and Milestones

GitHub issues and milestones are key tools for organizing and tracking tasks, bugs, and enhancements in a project. They help teams stay on top of project progress and prioritize work.

1. Managing Issues

Issues in GitHub allow you to track bugs, features, enhancements, and tasks. They serve as to-do lists and project management tools for developers. Each issue can have labels, assignees, milestones, and comments to help facilitate discussion.

- **Creating an Issue**:
    1. Navigate to the **"Issues"** tab of your repository.

2. Click on the **"New issue"** button.

3. Provide a title and a detailed description of the issue.

4. Optionally, assign labels (e.g., bug, enhancement), set the priority (using labels), and assign the issue to someone for resolution.

5. Submit the issue.

- **Using Labels**: Labels are used to categorize and filter issues, making it easier to organize them. Common labels include "bug", "enhancement", "help wanted", and "documentation". You can create custom labels specific to your project.

- **Assigning Issues**: Issues can be assigned to individual team members to indicate responsibility. This helps distribute tasks among contributors effectively.

- **Commenting on Issues**: You can comment on issues to discuss their status, ask questions, or provide additional context. This is especially useful for collaborating on bug fixes or feature requests.

2. Managing Milestones

Milestones help group issues and pull requests together to track progress toward a larger goal, such as a release version or a significant feature completion.

- **Creating a Milestone**:

1. Go to the **"Milestones"** tab in your repository.

2. Click on **"New milestone"**.

3. Provide a title, description, and due date (optional) for the milestone.

4. Add issues and pull requests to the milestone to track progress toward completion.

- **Closing Milestones**: When all issues in a milestone are closed, GitHub automatically closes the milestone and marks it as completed.

By combining issues and milestones, you can effectively plan and track your project's progress, ensuring that work is completed on schedule.

GitHub Pages: Creating Websites Directly from GitHub Repositories

GitHub Pages allows you to host static websites directly from a GitHub repository. This feature is commonly used for project documentation, portfolios, blogs, or personal websites.

1. Setting Up a GitHub Pages Site

To create a website using GitHub Pages, follow these steps:

1. **Create a GitHub Repository**:
   o If you don't already have one, create a new repository for your website.

2. **Create an `index.html` File**:

   - In your repository, create an `index.html` file in the root directory. This file will serve as the homepage for your site.

3. **Enable GitHub Pages**:

   - Navigate to the **"Settings"** tab of your repository.
   - Scroll down to the **GitHub Pages** section.
   - Under **Source**, select the branch you want to use (usually `main`) and the folder (root or `docs`).
   - GitHub will automatically generate a URL for your site: `https://username.github.io/repository-name/`.

4. **Custom Domain**:

   - If you want to use a custom domain (e.g., `www.mysite.com`), you can configure it in the **GitHub Pages** settings and add a `CNAME` file to your repository with your custom domain.

2. Adding Content to Your Website

- You can use simple HTML, CSS, and JavaScript to build your website. If you want to use more advanced features like templates, themes, or Jekyll (a static site generator), GitHub Pages has built-in support for it.

- If you want to use Jekyll, simply create a Jekyll template site and push the files to your repository. GitHub Pages will automatically generate your site using Jekyll.

GitHub Pages is a great tool for creating and hosting simple websites without the need for a backend server. It's particularly useful for hosting project documentation and personal websites.

Using GitHub Actions for Continuous Integration (CI)

GitHub Actions is a powerful feature for automating workflows and tasks, especially for Continuous Integration (CI) and Continuous Deployment (CD). With GitHub Actions, you can automate testing, building, and deploying your projects whenever code is pushed to your repository.

1. What is Continuous Integration (CI)?

Continuous Integration is the practice of automatically testing and building your code every time a change is made. This helps detect bugs early, ensures that the code works as expected, and saves time by automating repetitive tasks.

2. Setting Up GitHub Actions for CI

To set up CI using GitHub Actions, you need to define a **workflow** in a YAML file within your repository. Here's how you can do it:

1. **Create a Workflow File**:
   - In your repository, navigate to the `.github/workflows` directory.
   - Create a new YAML file (e.g., `ci.yml`).
   - This file will define your workflow, including when it should run (e.g., on push or pull request) and what actions it should take (e.g., run tests).

Example of a simple CI workflow file:

```yaml
name: CI Workflow

on:
  push:
    branches:
      - main
  pull_request:
    branches:
      - main

jobs:
  build:
    runs-on: ubuntu-latest
    steps:
      - name: Checkout repository
        uses: actions/checkout@v2
```

93

```
- name: Set up Node.js
  uses: actions/setup-node@v2
  with:
    node-version: '14'

- name: Install dependencies
  run: npm install

- name: Run tests
  run: npm test
```

In this example, the workflow runs on every push or pull request to the `main` branch, sets up Node.js, installs dependencies, and runs tests.

2. **GitHub Actions Logs**: Once the workflow is triggered, you can view the status of the actions in the **Actions** tab of your repository. You'll see logs that show which steps passed and which ones failed.

3. **Automating Deployment**: You can also use GitHub Actions to automate deployment to services like AWS, Azure, or Heroku. After passing tests, the workflow can deploy your code automatically.

Writing and Using GitHub Workflows

GitHub workflows are defined in YAML files and describe the steps that GitHub Actions should perform. Workflows can be simple or complex depending on the tasks they need to automate.

1. Workflow Syntax

- **name**:: Defines the name of the workflow (optional).
- **on**:: Specifies the events that trigger the workflow (e.g., push, `pull_request`, `release`).
- **jobs**:: Defines the different jobs in the workflow, and each job can have multiple steps.
- **runs-on**:: Specifies the environment for the job (e.g., `ubuntu-latest`, `windows-latest`).
- **steps**:: Lists the individual steps for the job, such as checking out the code, setting up dependencies, or running tests.

2. Example: Full Workflow for Node.js Project

Here's an example of a complete CI/CD workflow for a Node.js project:

```
yaml
```

```
name: Node.js CI/CD
```

```yaml
on:
  push:
    branches:
      - main
  pull_request:
    branches:
      - main

jobs:
  build:
    runs-on: ubuntu-latest

    steps:
      - name: Checkout code
        uses: actions/checkout@v2

      - name: Set up Node.js
        uses: actions/setup-node@v2
        with:
          node-version: '14'

      - name: Install dependencies
        run: npm install

      - name: Run tests
        run: npm test

  deploy:
    runs-on: ubuntu-latest
```

```
needs: build
steps:
  - name: Checkout code
    uses: actions/checkout@v2

  - name: Deploy to Server
    run: |
      ssh user@server "deploy_script.sh"
```

In this example, the workflow consists of two jobs:

1. **Build**: Runs the tests after installing dependencies.
2. **Deploy**: Deploys the code to a server after the tests pass.

3. Benefits of GitHub Actions

- **Automation**: Automates manual tasks like testing, building, and deployment.
- **Customizability**: You can write custom workflows for any task you want to automate.
- **Integration**: Easily integrates with many third-party services and cloud platforms.

Conclusion

In this chapter, we explored GitHub's advanced features that enable developers to manage projects more efficiently and automate repetitive tasks. You learned how to manage issues and milestones for tracking project progress, how to create websites using **GitHub Pages**, how to set up **Continuous Integration (CI)** using **GitHub Actions**, and how to write and use custom workflows to automate tasks in your repositories. Mastering these advanced features will allow you to take full advantage of GitHub's capabilities and streamline your development workflow.

CHAPTER 10

UNDERSTANDING AND RESOLVING GIT CONFLICTS

Merge conflicts are an inevitable part of collaborative software development. They occur when multiple developers make changes to the same part of a file or when Git cannot automatically reconcile differences between branches. In this chapter, we will explore the **types of merge conflicts**, **how they happen**, **tools for resolving conflicts**, and **best practices** to help avoid them.

Types of Merge Conflicts

Git conflicts typically occur in the following scenarios:

1. **Content Conflicts**:
   o This is the most common type of conflict, occurring when two branches modify the same lines in a file. Git cannot determine which version of the content should take precedence.
   o Example: Two developers edit the same line in a file (e.g., a function definition or a variable).
2. **Deletion Conflicts**:
   o A conflict occurs when one branch deletes a file while another branch modifies the same file. Git

99

cannot automatically determine whether to keep or delete the file.

- o Example: Developer A deletes a file, while Developer B edits it. Upon merging, Git will not know whether to delete the file or keep the changes.

3. **File Conflicts**:

- o Conflicts can also occur when a file is renamed or moved in one branch and edited in another. Git will be unable to automatically reconcile the changes.

- o Example: Developer A renames `file1.txt` to `file2.txt`, and Developer B modifies `file1.txt`. Git cannot know how to apply the changes to the renamed file.

How Conflicts Happen During Merges and Rebases

1. Merge Conflicts

A **merge conflict** happens when Git attempts to merge two branches and cannot automatically resolve the differences between the branches. Merge conflicts are common when you have two branches that have made conflicting changes to the same file or line of code.

- • **Example of a Merge Conflict**: Imagine two developers working on the same codebase. Developer A modifies line 10 of `example.txt`, and Developer B also modifies line 10 of the same file. When you attempt to merge the branches, Git cannot automatically decide which version of line 10 should be kept, resulting in a merge conflict.

- **How Merges Work**:
    1. When a conflict occurs, Git will stop and mark the conflicted files.
    2. You will need to manually resolve the conflict before proceeding with the merge.

2. Rebase Conflicts

A **rebase conflict** happens when you rebase your current branch onto another branch and Git cannot apply the commits from your branch onto the target branch. This is similar to a merge conflict, but it happens when you attempt to rebase instead of merge.

- **Example of a Rebase Conflict**: Suppose you're rebasing your feature branch onto `main`, but your changes conflict with the changes that have been made to `main` since you started working on your feature. Git will stop the rebase and ask you to resolve the conflicts before continuing.
- **How to Resolve Rebase Conflicts**:
    1. Git will stop the rebase process at the conflicting commit.
    2. You resolve the conflict in the same way as a merge conflict.

3. Once resolved, continue the rebase with `git rebase --continue`.

Tools for Resolving Conflicts

There are several tools that can help you resolve conflicts in Git. Some are built into Git itself, while others are third-party tools that provide a more graphical interface for resolving conflicts.

1. Git's Built-in Conflict Markers

Git automatically inserts conflict markers into files when a merge conflict occurs. These markers highlight the conflicting sections, and you need to manually edit the file to resolve the conflict.

- **Example of Conflict Markers**:

```cpp
<<<<<<< HEAD
// Changes from your current branch (e.g., main)
=======
// Changes from the branch being merged (e.g., feature-branch)
>>>>>>> feature-branch
```

- **Steps to Resolve with Conflict Markers**:
    1. Review the conflicting sections.

2. Edit the file to decide which changes to keep. You can:

- Keep changes from one branch.
- Merge both changes.
- Write a completely new solution.

3. Once you've resolved the conflict, remove the conflict markers (`<<<<<<<`, `=======`, and `>>>>>>>`).

4. Stage the file using `git add`, and then commit the changes.

2. Git GUI Tools

Many developers use GUI tools to help visualize and resolve conflicts. Popular Git GUI tools include:

- **Sourcetree**: A free Git GUI tool that shows conflicts clearly and allows you to resolve them using a visual interface.
- **GitKraken**: Another popular Git GUI with visual tools for managing conflicts, branches, and commits.

These tools allow you to resolve conflicts by providing a clear, side-by-side comparison of conflicting files, making it easier to decide which version to keep or how to merge the changes.

3. Third-Party Merge Tools

There are several third-party merge tools that you can configure Git to use for resolving conflicts. These tools typically offer advanced features like syntax highlighting, side-by-side comparisons, and conflict resolution buttons. Some of the most common merge tools include:

- **KDiff3**
- **Meld**
- **P4Merge**
- **Beyond Compare**

To configure a merge tool in Git, you can use the following command:

bash

```
git config --global merge.tool <tool-name>
```

For example, if you're using `meld`, the command would be:

bash

```
git config --global merge.tool meld
```

4. Visual Studio Code

If you use Visual Studio Code (VS Code) as your code editor, it has built-in Git support and an easy-to-use conflict resolution interface. VS Code displays conflict markers in the editor and provides buttons to accept incoming changes, current changes, or both.

You can open the conflicted file in VS Code and resolve the conflict directly within the editor.

Best Practices for Avoiding Conflicts

While conflicts are sometimes unavoidable, there are several best practices you can follow to minimize their occurrence and make them easier to resolve when they do happen.

1. Commit Frequently

Frequent commits allow you to identify conflicts early and make them easier to resolve. The more granular your commits, the easier it will be to spot and fix issues as they arise.

2. Pull and Merge Regularly

Regularly pulling changes from the main branch (or the branch you're working against) helps keep your branch up-to-date with the latest changes and minimizes the chance of conflicts later. You should merge or rebase frequently to stay in sync with the team's work.

- **Pulling Changes**:

```bash
git pull origin main
```

- **Rebasing Instead of Merging**: If you're working on a feature branch, regularly rebase your work onto the latest `main` to avoid complex merge conflicts later.

3. Work on Small, Focused Branches

Working on small, focused branches helps reduce the risk of conflicts. A small change is less likely to conflict with other parts of the codebase, and it's easier to merge back into the main branch.

4. Use Feature Flags

Feature flags (also known as feature toggles) allow you to deploy incomplete features without affecting the functionality of the application. By using feature flags, you can keep branches smaller and avoid long-lived feature branches, which can lead to more conflicts.

5. Communicate with Your Team

Good communication is key to avoiding conflicts. If multiple people are working on the same feature or code area, coordinate with your teammates. Let them know when you're working on a particular feature, and avoid working on the same parts of the code simultaneously.

6. Use Pull Requests for Collaboration

By using pull requests, you can review changes before they are merged into the main branch. This helps spot potential conflicts early and ensures that code is reviewed and tested before it becomes part of the main codebase.

7. Keep Branches Short-Lived

Long-lived branches are more likely to cause conflicts because they diverge further from the main codebase. Keep your feature branches short-lived to reduce the complexity of merging them back into the main branch.

In this chapter, we've discussed **merge conflicts**—what they are, why they happen, and how to resolve them. You learned how conflicts can arise during **merges** and **rebases**, the tools available for resolving conflicts (including Git's built-in conflict markers and third-party tools), and best practices for avoiding conflicts. By following these practices, you can streamline your Git workflow, reduce the frequency of conflicts, and resolve them quickly when they do occur.

CHAPTER 11

GIT HOOKS AND AUTOMATION

Git hooks are a powerful feature in Git that allow you to automate various tasks during the development workflow. They are scripts that Git automatically runs at certain points in the Git process. With Git hooks, you can enforce coding standards, run tests, or automate deployment steps, ensuring consistency and efficiency in your development process. In this chapter, we will explore **what Git hooks are**, **how to use them for automation**, **common Git hooks** like `pre-commit`, `pre-push`, and `post-commit`, and how to **automate workflows** using hooks.

What Are Git Hooks?

Git hooks are custom scripts that Git executes automatically before or after certain Git events, such as commits, pushes, merges, and checkouts. These hooks allow you to extend Git's functionality and integrate automated tasks into your workflow.

Git hooks are stored in the `.git/hooks/` directory of your repository. Each hook is a separate file that corresponds to a specific event. These hooks are written in plain shell script or any scripting language of your choice, such as Python, Ruby, or Node.js.

108

Types of Git Hooks:

- **Client-side hooks**: These hooks run on your local machine when you perform operations like committing, pushing, or merging.
- **Server-side hooks**: These hooks run on the Git server when it receives a request to perform operations like accepting pushes or accepting pull requests.

The most common hooks are triggered by actions like committing code, pushing code to a remote repository, or checking out a branch. Git provides a variety of hooks that you can configure and customize to suit your needs.

Using Git Hooks for Automation

Git hooks can automate a variety of tasks to improve your development workflow. Some examples include:

- **Running linters** to check code quality before committing.
- **Running tests** to ensure that your codebase is not broken.
- **Enforcing commit message guidelines** to ensure a consistent format for commit messages.
- **Automating deployments** after a successful commit or push.

By using Git hooks, you can integrate automated quality checks into the version control process, reducing manual effort and preventing errors from reaching the main codebase.

To enable or create a hook, navigate to the `.git/hooks/` directory in your repository. Git provides sample scripts with a `.sample` extension (e.g., `pre-commit.sample`). You can rename the script file and remove the `.sample` extension to activate the hook.

Common Git Hooks: `pre-commit, pre-push, post-commit`

Below, we'll discuss some of the most commonly used Git hooks and how they can be utilized in your workflow.

1. `pre-commit` Hook

The `pre-commit` hook runs before a commit is created. This hook is often used to ensure that code adheres to predefined quality standards, such as running linters or formatters.

- **Use Case**: You can use the `pre-commit` hook to:
    - Check for syntax errors or style violations.
    - Run tests to ensure the code passes basic checks before committing.
    - Automatically format code to conform to a style guide.

110

- **Example**: If you want to run a Python linter (e.g., `flake8`) before committing, you can add the following to your `pre-commit` script:

bash

```
#!/bin/sh
flake8 . --exit-zero
```

- **How to Enable**:
    1. Navigate to `.git/hooks/`.
    2. Rename the `pre-commit.sample` file to `pre-commit`.
    3. Edit the `pre-commit` file to add the necessary commands for your desired automation.

2. `pre-push` Hook

The `pre-push` hook is executed before changes are pushed to a remote repository. This hook allows you to validate the code before it is shared with others, ensuring that the changes meet the required standards.

- **Use Case**: Use the `pre-push` hook to:
    o Run tests to verify the correctness of the code.
    o Check for large files or secrets that shouldn't be pushed (e.g., `.env` files, sensitive keys).

111

o Block pushes that do not meet specific requirements.

- **Example**: To prevent pushing to a remote repository if any tests fail, you could add this script to your `pre-push` hook:

```bash
#!/bin/sh
npm test || { echo 'Tests failed. Push
aborted.'; exit 1; }
```

- **How to Enable**:
  1. Rename the `pre-push.sample` file to `pre-push`.
  2. Edit the `pre-push` file to include the necessary automation (e.g., running tests).

3. `post-commit` Hook

The `post-commit` hook runs immediately after a commit has been created. It is commonly used for actions that should occur after committing, such as sending notifications or triggering other processes.

- **Use Case**: You can use the `post-commit` hook to:
  o Send notifications (e.g., Slack, email) about the latest commit.

- o Trigger automated deployment or continuous integration processes.
- o Perform post-commit cleanup tasks (e.g., removing temporary files).

- **Example**: To send a notification after each commit, you can add the following to the `post-commit` hook:

```
bash
```

```
#!/bin/sh
echo "New commit created. Notifying team..."
curl -X POST -d "Commit message: $(git log -1 --pretty=%B)" https://api.notification-service.com
```

- **How to Enable**:
  1. Rename the `post-commit.sample` file to `post-commit`.
  2. Edit the `post-commit` file with your desired post-commit automation.

Automating Workflows with Hooks

Git hooks provide a seamless way to automate many tasks in your development workflow. By integrating Git hooks into your project, you can ensure that the development process remains consistent, errors are caught early, and deployments happen smoothly.

1. Automating Linting and Formatting

A common use case for Git hooks is to automate code linting and formatting. For example, you can set up a `pre-commit` hook to automatically run `eslint` or `prettier` on your code before committing it. This ensures that all code committed to the repository follows the correct style and format.

- **Example (pre-commit hook for JavaScript):**

```bash
#!/bin/sh
eslint . --fix
prettier --write .
```

2. Automating Testing

You can use Git hooks to ensure that your code passes tests before pushing it to a shared repository. This can prevent breaking changes from being introduced and improve the quality of your code.

- **Example (pre-push hook for running tests):**

```bash
```

```
#!/bin/sh
npm test || { echo 'Tests failed. Push
aborted.'; exit 1; }
```

3. Automating Deployment

You can automate deployments using Git hooks, particularly the `post-commit` or `post-push` hooks. For example, you can deploy your application to a server after each commit or push.

- **Example (post-push hook for deployment)**:

```
bash
```

```
#!/bin/sh
ssh user@server "deploy_script.sh"
```

4. Automating Version Bumping

Another useful automation task is bumping the version number in your project after a commit. You can automate this with a `post-commit` hook, updating the version number in `package.json` or any other versioning file.

- **Example (post-commit hook for version bump)**:

```
bash
```

```
#!/bin/sh
npm version patch
```

115

Conclusion

In this chapter, we covered **Git hooks**—custom scripts that allow you to automate and extend Git's functionality during various phases of your workflow. We explored **common hooks** such as `pre-commit`, `pre-push`, and `post-commit`, and learned how to use these hooks for automating tasks like linting, testing, deployment, and versioning. By leveraging Git hooks, you can streamline your development process, reduce human error, and ensure that your code meets the required standards before it's committed or pushed.

CHAPTER 12

MANAGING LARGE PROJECTS WITH GIT

Git is an essential tool for version control, even in the context of large-scale projects and teams. As projects grow in size, managing large repositories and coordinating work across large teams can become challenging. In this chapter, we will discuss how to effectively use Git in large teams and projects, the best practices for managing large repositories, the use of **submodules** and **subtrees** in Git, and how to handle **binary files** and large repositories using **Git LFS (Large File Storage)**.

Using Git in Large Teams and Projects

Git is a distributed version control system, making it highly suitable for collaboration among large teams. However, as the team and the project grow, so do the complexities of managing the repository. Here's how you can manage Git effectively in large teams and projects:

1. Organizing and Structuring Repositories

In large projects, it's important to organize your repository in a way that scales. This may involve:

- **Modularizing the project**: Breaking the project down into smaller, manageable sub-projects or components that can be worked on independently.

- **Using multiple repositories**: Instead of having one massive repository, consider using multiple smaller repositories for different components of the project. This helps reduce the load on a single repository, making it more maintainable and easier to work with.

2. Using Branching Strategies

With large teams, a well-defined branching strategy is essential. Some common strategies include:

- **GitFlow**: A widely used branching model that defines specific branches for feature development (`feature/`), releases (`release/`), and hotfixes (`hotfix/`).

- **GitHub Flow**: A simpler strategy where developers create feature branches from `main` and submit pull requests (PRs) to `main` for review and merging.

- **Trunk-Based Development**: A strategy where all developers commit directly to a single `main` branch (with small, frequent commits).

3. Efficient Code Reviews

With large teams, code reviews can become time-consuming. Use **Pull Requests (PRs)** to facilitate discussions around changes, and ensure that all code is reviewed before merging. Establish guidelines for writing clear commit messages, defining review standards, and handling feedback to improve efficiency.

4. Handling Merge Conflicts

In large projects, merge conflicts are inevitable, especially when multiple developers work on the same files. Regularly merging branches back into `main` and communicating with team members about ongoing work can help reduce conflicts. In case of conflicts, encourage frequent rebase or merge practice to keep the codebase consistent and avoid larger conflicts down the road.

Best Practices for Managing Large Repositories

Managing large repositories requires careful consideration to ensure the project remains maintainable and efficient. Here are some best practices for large repositories:

1. Limit the Size of Each Commit

Large commits that include many changes across different parts of the codebase can make it harder to review and understand the commit history. Keep commits small and focused, ideally addressing a single task, feature, or bug. This makes it easier to trace issues, roll back changes, and collaborate.

2. Use Tags and Releases

Tags are useful for marking significant points in the project's history, such as releases or milestones. Use tags to mark versions of your project that are ready for production or deployment. This makes it easy to track and roll back to specific versions of your codebase.

3. Avoid Storing Large Files in Git

Git is not well-suited for managing large files (e.g., images, videos, datasets, etc.) directly in the repository. Storing large files in Git can significantly increase the size of your repository and slow down performance.

4. Archive Old Branches

As the project evolves, some branches may become obsolete. To keep the repository clean and easy to navigate, archive or delete old feature branches that have been merged into the main branch.

5. Use a `.gitignore` File

Ensure that temporary files, build artifacts, and sensitive files are not accidentally committed to the repository. A `.gitignore` file allows you to define which files and directories Git should ignore. This keeps the repository clean and prevents unnecessary files from being tracked.

Submodules and Subtrees in Git

When managing large projects, you may encounter situations where certain parts of the codebase should be kept in separate repositories. Git provides two solutions for managing these situations: **submodules** and **subtrees**.

1. Git Submodules

A **submodule** is a Git repository embedded inside another Git repository. Submodules allow you to keep track of external libraries or dependencies as separate repositories within your project. This is useful for managing third-party dependencies that are maintained independently of your project.

- **Adding a Submodule**: To add a submodule to your repository, run:

```bash
git submodule add https://github.com/example/library.git path/to/submodule
git submodule update --init --recursive
```

- **Cloning a Repository with Submodules**: When cloning a repository with submodules, use:

```bash
git clone --recursive https://github.com/example/project.git
```

- **Updating Submodules**: To update a submodule to the latest commit, run:

```bash
git submodule update --remote
```

- **Advantages of Submodules**:
  - Keeps external dependencies in their own repository.
  - Ensures your main repository points to specific versions of the submodule.
- **Disadvantages of Submodules**:
  - Can be difficult to manage if there are frequent changes in the submodule or if multiple developers are involved.
  - Requires additional commands to clone, update, or work with submodules.

2. Git Subtrees

A **subtree** is an alternative to submodules for managing external repositories or projects inside a main repository. Unlike submodules, subtrees don't require separate commands to update or manage external repositories.

- **Adding a Subtree**: To add a subtree, run:

  bash

  ```
  git subtree add --prefix=path/to/subtree
  https://github.com/example/library.git
  master --squash
  ```

- **Pulling Changes from a Subtree**: To pull changes from the subtree's repository, use:

  bash

  ```
  git subtree pull --prefix=path/to/subtree
  https://github.com/example/library.git
  master --squash
  ```

- **Advantages of Subtrees**:
  - Easier to manage than submodules, as they don't require special commands.
  - Subtrees integrate better into the main repository, without the need for extra Git configuration.

123

- **Disadvantages of Subtrees**:
  - ○ It is more difficult to keep the subtree up to date if changes are frequent.
  - ○ Requires additional manual management of the history of the subtree repository.

Handling Binary Files and Large Repositories with Git LFS (Large File Storage)

Git is not optimized for storing large files, such as images, audio, video, and data files. Adding such files to your repository can cause the repository size to grow quickly, reducing performance and increasing storage costs. **Git Large File Storage (Git LFS)** is a solution to handle these large files efficiently.

What is Git LFS?

Git LFS is an extension for Git that replaces large files (e.g., images, audio, or binary files) with lightweight references in the Git repository. The actual content of these files is stored outside the repository, in an LFS server or cloud storage.

- **Why Use Git LFS?**
  - ○ **Reduce repository size**: Large files are stored separately, keeping the repository lightweight.
  - ○ **Improve performance**: Git LFS speeds up the clone and fetch operations by keeping large files out of the main repository.

124

How to Use Git LFS:

1. **Install Git LFS**:
   - Install Git LFS on your local machine. Instructions can be found on the Git LFS website.

2. **Initialize Git LFS**:
   - Run the following command to initialize Git LFS:

   bash

   ```
   git lfs install
   ```

3. **Track Large Files**:
   - You can track specific file types (e.g., .png, .mp4) by using the git lfs track command:

   bash

   ```
   git lfs track "*.png"
   git lfs track "*.mp4"
   ```

4. **Add and Commit Files**:
   - After tracking the large files, use the usual Git commands to add and commit the files:

   bash

   ```
   git add .gitattributes
   git add path/to/largefile.png
   ```

125

```
git commit -m "Add large files"
```

5. **Push to Remote Repository**:

   o When you push the changes to the remote repository, Git LFS will handle the large files and upload them to the LFS server.

   ```bash
   git push origin main
   ```

Benefits of Git LFS:

- **Efficient Storage**: Large files are stored separately, improving repository performance and reducing storage overhead.
- **Easy Integration**: Git LFS integrates seamlessly with Git and allows you to work with large files just like regular files.

Limitations of Git LFS:

- **Storage Costs**: Depending on the LFS service you use, there may be storage and bandwidth costs.
- **File Size Limits**: Some Git hosting platforms, like GitHub, impose limits on the size and number of files that can be managed with Git LFS.

126

In this chapter, we explored how to manage **large projects with Git**, including strategies for using Git in large teams, best practices for managing large repositories, and using **submodules** and **subtrees** to organize complex projects. We also discussed how to efficiently handle **binary files** and large repositories with **Git LFS**. By following these strategies and practices, you can scale Git effectively for large projects while maintaining high performance and flexibility.

CHAPTER 13

GIT BEST PRACTICES FOR DEVELOPERS

Git is a powerful tool that helps manage code changes, but its effectiveness largely depends on how it's used. Adopting best practices ensures that your Git history remains clean, understandable, and maintainable. In this chapter, we'll cover best practices for **commit messages**, maintaining a **clean Git history**, the importance of **atomic commits**, and the various **workflow strategies** that help teams collaborate efficiently.

Commit Message Guidelines: Writing Clear, Concise Messages

Commit messages are critical in providing context to your changes. They allow other developers (or even your future self) to understand why a change was made and what exactly was changed. Well-written commit messages help maintain a clean Git history, especially in large projects or teams.

1. Structure of a Good Commit Message

A commit message should typically follow a consistent structure to maximize clarity. Here's a widely used format:

- **Title (Subject line)**: A concise summary of the change, usually 50-72 characters.
- **Body (Description)**: An optional section for more detailed explanations or context. This section should be wrapped at 72 characters per line.
- **Footer**: Can include issue references or special instructions (e.g., breaking changes).

Example:

```
pgsql
```

```
Add user authentication feature

- Implement login and signup functionality.
- Use JWT tokens for session management.
- Update user model and database schema.

Closes #15
```

2. Best Practices for Writing Commit Messages

- **Use the imperative mood**: Write commit messages in the present tense (e.g., "Fix bug" rather than "Fixed bug").
- **Keep the title short but descriptive**: The subject should provide enough context to understand the change without needing to open the commit.
- **Explain "why" not just "what"**: While the title can describe what was changed, the body of the message

should explain why the change was necessary or how it solves a problem.

- **Separate different changes**: Each commit should focus on one logical change. If a commit does multiple things (e.g., refactoring and adding a new feature), it's better to split them into multiple commits.

By following these practices, you ensure that your commit messages remain meaningful and valuable for collaborators.

How to Maintain a Clean Git History

A clean Git history makes it easier for collaborators to understand the evolution of the project, track down bugs, and perform rollbacks if needed. Here are some practices to help maintain a clean history:

1. Use Descriptive Commit Messages

As we discussed earlier, writing clear, concise, and descriptive commit messages is vital for a clean Git history. Avoid generic messages like "Fix bug" or "Update code." Provide specific details about the change made.

2. Squash Small or Unnecessary Commits

Sometimes, you might make multiple small commits to address a single issue or feature. These commits may clutter the Git history.

Using `git rebase` or interactive rebasing (`git rebase -i`) to squash commits helps create a more meaningful history.

Example of squashing commits:

```bash
git rebase -i HEAD~3
```

In the interactive rebase interface, change `pick` to `squash` (or `s`) for the commits you want to combine.

3. Avoid Committing Unrelated Changes Together

Committing unrelated changes in a single commit can make it difficult to track down bugs or understand the context of a particular change. For instance, don't commit both a bug fix and a style update in the same commit. Instead, break them into separate, focused commits.

4. Keep Branches Short-Lived

Long-lived branches with many commits can make it hard to track changes and increase the likelihood of merge conflicts. Instead, create small, short-lived branches for individual features or bug fixes, and merge them back into the main branch frequently.

5. Use Rebase Instead of Merge (For Clean History)

When working on a feature branch, it's often beneficial to **rebase** your branch onto the main branch instead of merging it. Rebasing re-applies your commits on top of the latest `main` branch, preserving a linear commit history.

Example:

bash

```
git checkout feature-branch
git rebase main
```

This approach makes the commit history cleaner and easier to read since it avoids the clutter of merge commits.

6. Keep Your Commits Atomic

Atomic commits are commits that implement a single logical change. Atomic commits improve the readability of your Git history and make it easier to understand the purpose of each commit. Let's explore this in more detail next.

The Importance of Atomic Commits

An **atomic commit** is one that does one thing—no more, no less. The changes introduced by the commit should be logically coherent, making it easier to understand what was done, why it was done, and how to troubleshoot if something goes wrong.

Why Atomic Commits Matter:

1. **Ease of Reverting Changes**: If a commit introduces a bug or issue, it's easier to revert atomic commits since each commit addresses only one change or task.

2. **Simplifies Debugging**: When bugs are introduced, it's easier to pinpoint where and why they happened with atomic commits. It becomes simpler to isolate the problem in a specific commit.

3. **Better Collaboration**: When working in a team, atomic commits make it easier to review changes, as each commit is focused on a single purpose. Reviewers don't have to dig through unrelated changes to understand what the commit is doing.

4. **Improved History**: A clean, logical history makes it easier to track progress and generate changelogs for releases.

Examples of Atomic Commits:

- **Good**: "Add user authentication middleware"
- **Bad**: "Update user model and fix authentication bug"

The second example combines unrelated tasks (updating a model and fixing a bug) into one commit. The first example, however, is an atomic commit because it describes a single, focused change (adding middleware).

Workflow Strategies for Teams (Git Flow, GitHub Flow)

When working on a team, defining a clear Git workflow is essential to maintaining a consistent and organized project history. Several workflow strategies exist, each suitable for different types of projects. The two most popular workflows are **Git Flow** and **GitHub Flow**.

1. Git Flow

Git Flow is a well-defined branching model that was introduced by Vincent Driessen. It uses multiple branches for managing different stages of the development lifecycle (e.g., feature development, releases, and hotfixes).

Main branches in Git Flow:

- `main`: The main production-ready branch.
- `develop`: The branch where all features are merged before a release.

Supporting branches in Git Flow:

- **Feature branches**: Used for developing new features. These branches are created off `develop`.

134

- **Release branches**: Created from `develop` when preparing for a release. They allow for final bug fixes and version number changes before merging into `main`.
- **Hotfix branches**: Used to address urgent issues in the production code. These branches are created from `main`.

Workflow Example:

1. Create a feature branch: `git checkout -b feature/user-authentication develop`.
2. After completing the feature, merge it into `develop`.
3. Create a release branch when preparing for deployment: `git checkout -b release/v1.0 develop`.
4. Once the release is stable, merge it into `main` and tag the release.
5. For urgent fixes, create a hotfix branch from `main`.

Git Flow is a great choice for teams working on large projects with multiple release cycles.

2. GitHub Flow

GitHub Flow is a simpler, more streamlined workflow, designed for projects that deploy frequently or continuously (e.g., web applications). GitHub Flow is based on the concept of using pull requests for code reviews and direct collaboration.

Main branches in GitHub Flow:

135

- **main**: The main branch, which is always in a deployable state.

Workflow Example:

1. Create a feature branch from `main`: `git checkout -b feature/user-authentication main`.
2. Work on the feature and commit changes to the feature branch.
3. Push the feature branch to GitHub: `git push origin feature/user-authentication`.
4. Open a pull request (PR) to merge the feature branch into `main`.
5. After code review and testing, merge the pull request into `main`.
6. Deploy the changes to production immediately.

GitHub Flow is ideal for teams that prefer continuous deployment and need a simple, flexible workflow.

Conclusion

In this chapter, we covered Git best practices for developers, including **commit message guidelines**, **maintaining a clean Git history**, and the importance of **atomic commits**. We also explored popular **workflow strategies** like **Git Flow** and **GitHub Flow**, which help teams collaborate effectively. By following these practices, you can ensure that your Git workflow remains efficient, your codebase stays organized, and your project's history is easy to navigate and understand. Implementing these best practices will help you and your team work together seamlessly while maintaining a high-quality codebase.

CHAPTER 14

GIT AND OPEN SOURCE CONTRIBUTION

Open-source software development is built on collaboration, with developers from around the world contributing to shared projects. GitHub plays a pivotal role in facilitating open-source contributions by providing a platform for version control, collaboration, and code sharing. In this chapter, we'll explore **how to contribute to open-source projects using GitHub**, including **forking and cloning repositories**, **best practices for submitting pull requests**, and understanding **contribution guidelines** and **etiquette**.

Contributing to Open-Source Projects Using GitHub

Contributing to open-source projects not only helps improve the software but also allows you to learn, collaborate with other developers, and build your programming portfolio. GitHub is the most widely used platform for open-source projects, and it makes it easy to collaborate by providing tools like issues, pull requests, and project management features.

Steps to Contribute:

1. **Find a Project**: The first step is to find an open-source project you'd like to contribute to. GitHub's Explore page, issue trackers, and topics (e.g., "good first issue") are great starting points.

2. **Fork the Repository**: Once you find a project, fork it to your GitHub account. Forking creates a personal of the repository where you can freely make changes without affecting the original project.

3. **Clone the Repository**: After forking the repository, clone it to your local machine to start working on it.

4. **Make Changes**: Create a new branch for your changes, whether it's fixing a bug, adding a feature, or improving documentation.

5. **Commit and Push**: After making changes, commit them with a clear message and push them to your forked repository on GitHub.

6. **Submit a Pull Request**: Once your changes are pushed to your fork, open a pull request (PR) to propose your changes to the original repository.

7. **Review and Feedback**: The maintainers will review your pull request, provide feedback, and may suggest further changes. Once the PR is approved, it will be merged into the main repository.

Forking and Cloning Repositories for Contributions

When contributing to an open-source project, you often need to fork and clone repositories. Here's how these steps work:

1. Forking a Repository

- **What is Forking?**: Forking creates a of the original repository under your own GitHub account. This allows you to freely make changes to the repository without affecting the original project.
- **How to Fork a Repository**:
    1. Go to the repository you want to contribute to on GitHub.
    2. Click the **"Fork"** button at the top-right of the page.
    3. GitHub will create a of the repository in your GitHub account.

2. Cloning a Repository

- **What is Cloning?**: Cloning downloads a local of the repository to your computer. This is where you can make changes, test them, and commit them before pushing them back to GitHub.
- **How to Clone a Repository**:
    1. After forking the repository, go to your forked repository's GitHub page.

2. Click the **"Code"** button and the URL (either HTTPS or SSH).

3. Open your terminal and run the following command to clone the repository:

```bash

git                                    clone
https://github.com/yourusername/rep
ository.git
```

- Now, you have the repository on your local machine, and you can start making changes.

Best Practices for Submitting Pull Requests to Open-Source Projects

Once you've made changes and are ready to submit them, the next step is to create a pull request. The pull request is your way of proposing the changes to the original repository. Here are best practices to follow when submitting a pull request:

1. Follow the Project's Contribution Guidelines

Most open-source projects have **contribution guidelines** that provide instructions on how to contribute to the project. These guidelines may include coding standards, commit message formats, and testing requirements. Be sure to read and follow these guidelines before submitting your changes.

- **Where to Find Contribution Guidelines**: Look for a CONTRIBUTING.md file in the project's repository or check the README for any specific instructions for contributors.

2. Work on a Separate Branch

Always create a new branch for the changes you intend to make. Do not make changes directly on the main branch, as this can cause conflicts and make it harder to manage contributions.

- **How to Create a New Branch**:

bash

```
git checkout -b my-feature-branch
```

- **Why Use a Separate Branch?**
  - **Clean History**: It keeps your commit history organized and separates your work from the main branch.
  - **Easy Collaboration**: It allows multiple contributors to work on the same repository without overwriting each other's work.

3. Keep Commits Small and Focused

Each commit should address a specific change or bug fix. This makes it easier for reviewers to understand your changes and ensures that each commit has a clear purpose.

- **Example of Good Commit Messages**:
  - "Fix typo in user authentication documentation."
  - "Add tests for the new login endpoint."

4. Test Your Changes Before Submitting

Before submitting your pull request, ensure that your changes work correctly by testing them in your local environment. If the project includes automated tests, run them to verify that everything passes.

- **Running Tests**: If the project has a testing framework (e.g., `npm test` for Node.js projects), run the tests to ensure nothing is broken.

5. Provide a Clear and Descriptive Pull Request Message

When you create a pull request, include a clear description of what the pull request does. Reference the issue number if it relates to an open issue.

- **Example of a Pull Request Description**:

143

```
bash
```

```
## Description
This PR fixes the login issue where users
were unable to authenticate using OAuth. It
modifies the authentication middleware to
properly handle the OAuth response.
```

```
## Related Issue
Closes #45
```

6. Be Open to Feedback and Make Changes

After submitting a pull request, project maintainers or other contributors will review your code. They may suggest improvements or ask for changes. Be open to feedback and make any requested changes promptly.

- **How to Update a Pull Request**:
    1. Make the necessary changes in your local branch.
    2. Commit the changes and push them to your fork:

    ```
    bash
    ```

    ```
    git commit -m "Fix typo in
    authentication logic"
    git push origin my-feature-branch
    ```

7. Keep Pull Requests Focused

Each pull request should focus on a single issue or feature. Avoid submitting large, multi-feature pull requests. Breaking your contributions into smaller, manageable pieces will make them easier to review and merge.

Understanding Contribution Guidelines and Etiquette

Most open-source projects follow certain **etiquette** and **guidelines** to ensure contributions are high quality and well-managed. Here are some key points to keep in mind:

1. Read the README and Contribution Guidelines

Before starting any work, make sure you read the repository's **README** and **CONTRIBUTING.md** files. These documents provide important information about the project, including the coding standards, commit message format, and how to set up your local environment.

2. Engage with the Community

Many open-source projects have a community around them, and it's important to engage respectfully with other contributors. If you have a question or need clarification, consider opening an **issue** to ask for help rather than jumping straight into submitting a pull request.

- **Engage in Discussions**: Use the GitHub discussion threads or comments to communicate with the maintainers and other contributors.
- **Be Respectful**: Open-source communities thrive on respect and collaboration. Always be polite and constructive when discussing issues or giving feedback.

3. Understand the License

Most open-source projects are licensed under specific open-source licenses (e.g., MIT, GPL). Make sure you understand the terms of the license, especially when it comes to redistribution and contributions.

4. Acknowledge and Follow Code of Conduct

Many open-source projects have a **Code of Conduct** to ensure a welcoming and inclusive environment. Read and follow the code of conduct to help maintain a positive atmosphere in the community.

Conclusion

Contributing to open-source projects is a rewarding way to improve your skills, collaborate with others, and contribute to the global software community. By following the right procedures— **forking and cloning repositories, submitting clear and concise pull requests**, and respecting **contribution guidelines and**

etiquette—you can ensure that your contributions are effective and well-received. Open-source contribution is not just about coding but also about communicating, learning, and working together to build something valuable.

CHAPTER 15

GIT AND CI/CD INTEGRATION

Continuous Integration (CI) and Continuous Deployment (CD) are practices that allow software development teams to deliver code changes frequently and reliably. By automating testing, integration, and deployment, CI/CD ensures that software is always in a deployable state, reducing the chances of bugs and improving code quality. In this chapter, we will explore **what CI/CD is**, how **Git integrates with CI/CD tools**, how to **set up CI pipelines** using **GitHub Actions**, and how to **automate deployments** to streamline your development process.

What is Continuous Integration and Continuous Deployment (CI/CD)?

1. Continuous Integration (CI)

Continuous Integration is the practice of automatically integrating code changes into a shared repository frequently, often multiple times a day. Each time code is pushed to the repository, the CI system automatically runs tests and checks to verify that the code integrates successfully and does not break the application.

Key Aspects of CI:

- **Automated Testing**: Every time a change is made, automated tests are run to ensure that no existing functionality is broken and that the new code behaves as expected.
- **Frequent Merges**: Developers regularly commit code to the main branch, avoiding large, conflicting merges in the future.
- **Faster Feedback**: Developers get immediate feedback on their changes, which helps them fix issues early in the development cycle.

2. Continuous Deployment (CD)

Continuous Deployment takes CI a step further by automatically deploying code changes to a production or staging environment after passing tests. This ensures that every change that passes CI is immediately pushed to production, keeping the software always up to date.

Key Aspects of CD:

- **Automated Deployment**: Once the code passes all automated tests, it is deployed automatically, without manual intervention.
- **Faster Releases**: New features and bug fixes reach users faster, improving the overall software delivery lifecycle.

- **Reduced Risk**: By deploying frequently in small increments, the risk of large-scale failures is reduced.

In practice, many teams combine both CI and CD, where CI ensures the integrity of the codebase and CD automatically deploys changes to production or staging environments.

Using Git with CI/CD Tools like Jenkins, CircleCI, and GitHub Actions

Several CI/CD tools are available for automating testing and deployment. Below are some popular CI/CD tools that integrate with Git:

1. Jenkins

Jenkins is an open-source automation server commonly used to set up and manage CI/CD pipelines. It can integrate with Git repositories and automatically trigger builds when code changes are pushed to a repository.

- **How Jenkins Works with Git**:
  - Jenkins is set up to listen to changes in the Git repository. When a new commit is pushed, Jenkins can automatically trigger the build process, run tests, and deploy the changes if successful.
- **Advantages of Jenkins**:

- o **Highly customizable**: Jenkins supports many plugins, making it adaptable to a wide variety of workflows and integrations.
- o **Wide community support**: Jenkins has a large ecosystem of plugins and integrations.

2. CircleCI

CircleCI is a cloud-based CI/CD service that automates the process of testing and deploying code. It integrates with GitHub and GitLab, automatically running tests and deploying code when changes are detected.

- **How CircleCI Works with Git**:
  - o CircleCI is connected to your GitHub repository, and whenever a new commit is made, it triggers a CircleCI workflow to run tests and, if they pass, deploy the code.
- **Advantages of CircleCI**:
  - o **Fast and scalable**: CircleCI's cloud-based solution provides fast processing and is highly scalable for large teams.
  - o **Parallelism**: It can run multiple jobs simultaneously to speed up build times.

3. GitHub Actions

GitHub Actions is a CI/CD and automation tool built into GitHub that allows you to automate workflows directly in your GitHub repository. It allows you to define custom workflows for CI/CD pipelines using simple YAML configuration files.

- **How GitHub Actions Works with Git**:
  - o GitHub Actions is natively integrated with GitHub, so it's perfect for automating workflows like testing, building, and deploying code directly from your repository.
  - o You define workflows using YAML files that specify when a workflow should run (e.g., on push, pull request, or on a scheduled interval).
- **Advantages of GitHub Actions**:
  - o **Native integration with GitHub**: GitHub Actions is tightly integrated with GitHub repositories, simplifying the CI/CD process for developers already using GitHub.
  - o **Free tier available**: GitHub offers free usage of GitHub Actions for public repositories, with generous limits for private repositories as well.
  - o **Custom workflows**: You can define workflows for any process in the software development lifecycle, including running tests, building the project, deploying to production, and more.

Setting Up CI Pipelines with GitHub Actions

GitHub Actions makes it easy to set up continuous integration pipelines. Here's how you can configure a basic CI pipeline using GitHub Actions:

1. Creating a Workflow File

1. Inside your GitHub repository, navigate to the `.github/workflows/` directory. If this directory doesn't exist, create it.
2. Create a new YAML file, for example, `ci.yml`, to define your CI pipeline.

2. Defining a Workflow

A basic example of a CI pipeline for a Node.js project could look like this:

```yaml
name: Node.js CI

on:
  push:
    branches:
      - main
  pull_request:
    branches:
```

```
      - main

jobs:
  build:
    runs-on: ubuntu-latest

    steps:
      - name: Checkout repository
        uses: actions/checkout@v2

      - name: Set up Node.js
        uses: actions/setup-node@v2
        with:
          node-version: '14'

      - name: Install dependencies
        run: npm install

      - name: Run tests
        run: npm test
```

- **Explanation of the Workflow**:
  - **on:**: Specifies when the workflow should run. In this case, it runs on `push` and `pull_request` to the `main` branch.
  - **jobs:**: Defines the jobs within the workflow. Here, we have a `build` job that runs on an Ubuntu environment.

154

○ **steps**:: Defines the steps for the job. The steps here include checking out the code, setting up Node.js, installing dependencies, and running tests.

3. Pushing the Workflow File

Once you've created the workflow file and committed it to your repository, GitHub Actions will automatically detect the file and trigger the workflow when the defined events occur (such as a push to `main`).

4. Viewing Workflow Results

After a workflow runs, you can view its status on the **Actions** tab of your GitHub repository. You'll see whether the workflow passed or failed and can drill down into the logs for each step.

Deploying Code Changes Automatically Using GitHub

GitHub Actions can also handle Continuous Deployment (CD) by automating the process of deploying code to production or staging environments after it has passed all tests.

1. Example: Deploying to Heroku

Here's an example of how to set up a deployment workflow to automatically deploy a Node.js app to **Heroku** when changes are pushed to `main`:

```yaml
name: Deploy to Heroku

on:
  push:
    branches:
      - main

jobs:
  deploy:
    runs-on: ubuntu-latest

    steps:
      - name: Checkout repository
        uses: actions/checkout@v2

      - name: Set up Node.js
        uses: actions/setup-node@v2
        with:
          node-version: '14'

      - name: Install dependencies
```

```
    run: npm install


  - name: Deploy to Heroku
    run: |
      git        remote        add        heroku
https://git@heroku.com/your-app.git
      git push heroku main
    env:
      HEROKU_API_KEY:                        ${{
secrets.HEROKU_API_KEY }}
```

In this example:

- The `push` event triggers the deployment when code is pushed to the `main` branch.
- After installing dependencies, the `git push heroku main` command pushes the code to Heroku.

2. Using GitHub Secrets for Secure Deployment

GitHub Actions allows you to store sensitive information (like API keys) securely using **GitHub Secrets**. In the example above, `HEROKU_API_KEY` is stored as a secret and used in the deployment process.

To add secrets:

1. Go to your repository's **Settings**.

2. Under **Secrets** in the left sidebar, click **New repository secret**.

3. Add your Heroku API key or other sensitive information as a secret.

Conclusion

In this chapter, we discussed the importance of **Continuous Integration (CI)** and **Continuous Deployment (CD)** in modern software development. We learned how to use **Git with CI/CD tools** like **Jenkins**, **CircleCI**, and **GitHub Actions** to automate testing, integration, and deployment workflows. GitHub Actions provides a powerful and flexible way to automate your development process directly within GitHub, making it easy to set up CI pipelines and deploy code changes automatically. By integrating CI/CD into your workflow, you can ensure faster, more reliable software delivery and reduce the risk of bugs in production.

CHAPTER 16

GIT TAGGING AND RELEASES

Git tags are a powerful feature that allows you to mark specific points in the history of your repository, often to signify important events like releases or milestones. By using tags, you can easily refer to particular commits without having to remember commit hashes. In this chapter, we will dive into **Git tagging**, explore the differences between **lightweight** and **annotated tags**, show you how to **create and manage tags**, and discuss how to use tags for **versioning and releases**. Additionally, we will cover how to **automate releases** with **GitHub Releases**.

Understanding Git Tags: Lightweight vs Annotated Tags

Git tags are essentially markers that point to a specific commit in the Git history. There are two types of tags in Git: **lightweight tags** and **annotated tags**. Each serves different purposes and has unique characteristics.

1. Lightweight Tags

A **lightweight tag** is essentially a pointer to a specific commit. It does not contain any extra information, such as the tagger's name or the date it was created. It's the simplest type of tag.

- **Characteristics**:

    o It's just a reference to a commit.

    o It's fast and doesn't involve any additional metadata.

    o It's essentially a bookmark in the repository history.

- **When to Use**: Lightweight tags are typically used when you need a quick and simple way to mark a commit, without needing to attach any additional metadata like version numbers or release notes.

- **Creating a Lightweight Tag**: To create a lightweight tag, use the following command:

```bash
git tag v1.0.0
```

2. Annotated Tags

An **annotated tag** is a full object in the Git database. It contains more information, such as the tagger's name, email, date, and a message. Annotated tags are often used to mark important points in the history, such as release versions.

- **Characteristics**:

    o Contains metadata like the tagger's name, email, date, and a message.

    o Is stored as a full object in the Git database.

- o Is more suitable for marking releases or other significant milestones in your project.

- **When to Use**: Annotated tags should be used for marking releases, major milestones, or any significant points in your project's history, as they provide more information and can be signed with GPG for added security.

- **Creating an Annotated Tag**: To create an annotated tag, use the following command:

```bash

git tag -a v1.0.0 -m "First official release"
```

The -a flag specifies that it is an annotated tag, and -m allows you to add a message.

Difference Between Lightweight and Annotated Tags

Feature	Lightweight Tag	Annotated Tag
Contains metadata	No	Yes (name, email, date, message)
Stored as a full object	No	Yes

Feature	Lightweight Tag	Annotated Tag
Use case	Quick marks or bookmarks	Releases, milestones, important points
Can be signed with GPG	No	Yes
Examples	Marking a temporary point	Version releases

Creating and Managing Tags with Git

Now that we understand the two types of tags, let's explore how to **create**, **list**, and **delete** tags in Git.

1. Creating a Tag

As mentioned earlier, you can create both lightweight and annotated tags. The basic command for creating a tag is:

- **Lightweight Tag**:

```bash

git tag v1.0.0
```

- **Annotated Tag**:

```bash

```

```
git tag -a v1.0.0 -m "Release version
1.0.0"
```

2. Listing Tags

You can list all tags in your repository using the following command:

```
bash
```

```
git tag
```

If you want to list tags that match a specific pattern (e.g., all tags starting with v1.), you can use:

```
bash
```

```
git tag -l "v1.*"
```

3. Viewing Tag Details

To view the details of an annotated tag (e.g., the message and metadata), use the following command:

```
bash
```

```
git show v1.0.0
```

This will show the commit the tag points to, along with any metadata and the tag message.

163

4. Deleting Tags

If you need to delete a tag, use the following command:

- **Delete a Tag Locally**:

  bash

  ```
  git tag -d v1.0.0
  ```

- **Delete a Tag on a Remote**: If you've pushed the tag to a remote repository and want to delete it there, use the following:

  bash

  ```
  git push --delete origin v1.0.0
  ```

5. Pushing Tags to Remote Repositories

By default, tags are not automatically pushed when you push branches to a remote repository. To push tags to the remote, you can either push individual tags or all tags at once:

- **Push a Single Tag**:

  bash

  ```
  git push origin v1.0.0
  ```

164

- **Push All Tags**:

```bash
bash
```

```bash
git push --tags
```

Using Tags for Versioning and Releases

Tags are commonly used for versioning in Git repositories. By tagging specific commits, you can indicate stable versions of your code, making it easier to roll back to a previous state or track the history of releases.

1. Versioning with Tags

Versioning helps track the progress of a project and allows developers to mark significant changes, such as new features or bug fixes. A common convention is to use **semantic versioning** (e.g., v1.0.0, v1.1.0, v2.0.0), which follows the format:

- **Major version**: Significant changes that may break compatibility.
- **Minor version**: Backward-compatible new features or improvements.
- **Patch version**: Bug fixes and patches.

By tagging releases with version numbers, you create a clear, accessible history of how the project has evolved.

2. Creating Release Tags

When you're ready to mark a new release, create an annotated tag with a version number, then push it to the remote repository:

bash

```
git tag -a v1.2.0 -m "Release version 1.2.0:
Added new features and bug fixes"
git push origin v1.2.0
```

This allows you and your collaborators to refer to specific releases easily and helps in tracking project milestones.

Automating Releases with GitHub Releases

GitHub provides a feature called **GitHub Releases** that allows you to create a formal release of your project directly from GitHub. Releases are tied to Git tags, and you can include release notes and binaries (e.g., compiled code, assets) for each release.

1. Creating a GitHub Release

To create a release on GitHub, follow these steps:

1. **Tag Your Code**:
   - o Make sure your code is tagged (either manually or through a CI/CD pipeline).
   - o Use the command:

166

```
bash
```

```
git tag -a v1.0.0 -m "Release v1.0.0"
```

2. **Push the Tag to GitHub**:

```
bash
```

```
git push origin v1.0.0
```

3. **Create the Release**:
   - o Go to your repository on GitHub and click on the **Releases** tab.
   - o Click on **"Draft a new release"**.
   - o Select the tag you just pushed (e.g., v1.0.0).
   - o Add a release title and description (release notes).
   - o Optionally, you can attach binary files or compiled assets for your release.
   - o Click **"Publish release"** to make the release available to others.

2. Automating Releases with GitHub Actions

You can automate the release process using **GitHub Actions**, which allows you to trigger the creation of releases automatically based on certain events (e.g., when a new tag is pushed).

Here's an example of an automated release workflow in GitHub Actions:

167

```yaml
yaml

name: Release

on:
  push:
    tags:
      - 'v*.*.*'

jobs:
  release:
    runs-on: ubuntu-latest
    steps:
      - name: Checkout code
        uses: actions/checkout@v2
      - name: Create GitHub Release
        uses: gh-actions/create-release@v1
        with:
          tag_name: ${{ github.ref }}
          release_name: Release ${{ github.ref }}
          body: |
            This release includes the following changes:
              - Feature 1
              - Bug Fixes
        env:
          GITHUB_TOKEN: ${{ secrets.GITHUB_TOKEN }}
```

This GitHub Actions workflow creates a release automatically every time a tag that starts with v is pushed. The release includes the tag name, release name, and release notes.

Conclusion

In this chapter, we covered the key concepts of **Git tagging and releases**. You learned the difference between **lightweight** and **annotated tags**, how to **create and manage tags**, and how to use tags for **versioning and marking releases** in your project. We also explored how to **automate releases using GitHub Actions** and create formal **GitHub Releases** that include binaries, release notes, and other assets. By mastering Git tags and releases, you can effectively manage your project's versioning, ensure smooth releases, and automate the deployment process.

CHAPTER 17

GIT FOR VERSIONING DATABASES

Managing and versioning database schemas and data are crucial components of software development, especially when working with large applications or teams. Git can be an invaluable tool for tracking changes to your database schema and data, just as it is for tracking code changes. In this chapter, we will explore how to **manage database schemas with Git**, handle **database migrations with version control**, version **data in large applications**, and follow **best practices** for working with database changes in Git.

Managing Database Schema with Git

Database schema changes, such as modifying tables, adding columns, or changing constraints, are an integral part of many development processes. These changes should be tracked and versioned just like code to ensure that database changes are consistent across environments (development, staging, production) and teams.

1. Storing Database Schema Files in Git

To manage your database schema using Git, it's common to store schema definitions in SQL or migration files in your repository. This allows you to track changes, roll back to previous versions, and share updates with the team.

- **Storing Schema Files**: Store SQL files that define your schema (e.g., create_tables.sql, alter_schema.sql, etc.) in your Git repository. These files should contain all the necessary changes to modify the database schema.

- **Example**: Suppose you want to create a table for user data. You can create a file called create_users_table.sql and include the SQL commands to define the table structure:

sql

```
CREATE TABLE users (
    id INT PRIMARY KEY,
    name VARCHAR(255) NOT NULL,
    email VARCHAR(255) NOT NULL,
    created_at       TIMESTAMP       DEFAULT
CURRENT_TIMESTAMP
);
```

- **Tracking Schema Changes in Git**: Every time you change the database schema, create a new SQL file or update the existing one, and commit these changes to your Git repository:

```bash
git add create_users_table.sql
git commit -m "Add users table"
git push origin main
```

2. Versioning Schema Changes

Schema changes should be versioned and tagged with clear commit messages, just as you would with code. Each change to the schema (whether it's adding a table, changing a column type, or adding an index) should be tracked with its own commit.

- **Example of Versioned Schema Files**:
  - o v1_create_users_table.sql
  - o v2_add_index_to_users_email.sql
  - o v3_alter_users_add_last_login_colum
    n.sql

By versioning your database schema files, you can keep track of all changes made to the database and ensure that everyone is working with the correct schema version.

Handling Database Migrations with Version Control

Database migrations are the process of applying changes to the database schema in a consistent manner across different environments. This includes adding, removing, or modifying tables, columns, and constraints. Git can be used to version these migrations and ensure they are applied in a controlled way.

1. What are Database Migrations?

A **migration** is a script or set of scripts that modifies the database schema. Migrations provide a way to evolve the schema over time while maintaining backward compatibility and enabling easy rollbacks.

- **Example of a Migration**: Suppose you're adding a profile_picture column to the users table. A migration file might look like this:

  sql

  ```
  ALTER TABLE users ADD COLUMN profile_picture VARCHAR(255);
  ```

2. Using Migration Tools with Git

To manage migrations effectively, many developers use migration tools like **Liquibase**, **Flyway**, or the **Rails Active Record Migration** system. These tools allow you to write migrations that are automatically versioned and can be applied in a controlled manner across multiple environments.

- **Example of a Rails Migration**: Rails migrations use Ruby scripts to define schema changes. When you generate a migration in Rails, it creates a timestamped file like:

```ruby
class       AddProfilePictureToUsers        <
ActiveRecord::Migration[6.0]
  def change
    add_column  :users,  :profile_picture,
:string
  end
end
```

- **Tracking Migrations with Git**: Migrations should be committed to Git in the same way as schema files. Every time a migration is created, it should be added and pushed to the repository:

```bash
git                                      add
db/migrate/20220101_add_profile_picture_t
o_users.rb
```

```
git commit -m "Add profile_picture column
to users table"
git push origin main
```

3. Applying Migrations in Different Environments

Once migrations are tracked in Git, you can apply them in different environments (e.g., local development, staging, production) to keep the database schema in sync.

- **Applying Migrations**:
  - In Rails, you can apply the migration using:

    ```bash
    bin/rails db:migrate
    ```

  - In Flyway, migrations are applied automatically when the application starts.

- **Rolling Back Migrations**:
  - If something goes wrong, you can roll back the last migration in Rails with:

    ```bash
    bin/rails db:rollback
    ```

By using migration tools with Git, you ensure that all developers and environments apply the same set of changes in the correct order.

Versioning Data in Large Applications

Versioning database data is more complex than versioning schema changes. While schema changes are typically tracked with SQL scripts, managing and versioning data itself can be tricky, especially in large applications.

1. Using Database Seeds and Fixtures

To handle versioned data, many developers use **seed** or **fixture** files, which are data files that can be committed to Git to set up or reset the database state. These files can contain sample data, default values, or testing data that are useful during development or testing.

- **Database Seed Example** (Rails): A `seeds.rb` file in Rails might look like this:

```ruby
```

```
User.create(name:    'John    Doe',    email:
'john@example.com')
```

- **Fixture Files**: Some applications use fixture files (e.g., JSON, CSV, or YAML files) to load data into the database. These files can be versioned in Git and used to populate the database when needed.

2. Handling Large Data Changes

In large applications, handling large datasets requires more careful consideration. Rather than committing large data files directly to Git, consider using the following approaches:

- **Data Migrations**: Use SQL scripts or database migration tools to migrate large datasets between versions.
- **Database Snapshots**: In some cases, database snapshots (e.g., exporting and importing large data sets) can be used to handle large-scale data migrations.

3. Managing Data Versioning with Git LFS

For very large data files, such as binary files or large datasets, consider using **Git LFS** (Large File Storage). Git LFS stores large files outside of Git while keeping references to them inside the repository. This ensures that your repository remains lightweight and Git performance is not compromised.

- **How Git LFS Works**: Git LFS replaces large files in your repository with small pointers that reference the actual files stored outside of Git. You can use Git LFS for storing large assets, such as images, videos, or database dumps.

Best Practices for Working with Database Changes in Git

Managing database changes effectively in Git requires discipline and attention to detail. Here are some best practices to follow:

1. Use Migration Tools for Consistency

Use migration tools like **Liquibase**, **Flyway**, or Rails migrations to ensure database changes are applied in a consistent and repeatable manner. These tools help avoid manual errors and ensure the database schema is always in sync across all environments.

2. Keep Migrations Small and Incremental

Each migration should contain a single change to the schema or data. This makes it easier to track, test, and roll back changes. Avoid large migrations that introduce multiple changes at once.

3. Test Migrations Locally Before Pushing

Before pushing migrations to Git and applying them in staging or production, test them in a local environment. This ensures that the migrations work as expected and minimizes the risk of errors in production.

4. Version Control Database Seed and Fixture Files

Use seed or fixture files to track and version data that is needed for development or testing. Avoid committing large volumes of production data, and use data dumps sparingly.

5. Use Git LFS for Large Data Files

For large datasets, images, or binary files, use **Git LFS** to store the data outside of Git. This ensures your repository remains fast and efficient while still allowing you to version large data assets.

6. Write Clear Commit Messages for Database Changes

Just like with code changes, write clear and descriptive commit messages for database changes. Include details about what the migration does and any additional context about why the change was made.

Conclusion

In this chapter, we explored how to effectively use Git for versioning database schemas, managing migrations, handling large datasets, and following best practices for database changes in version control. By using migration tools, committing schema and data changes in an organized way, and automating database

179

management with Git, you can ensure that your database remains consistent, maintainable, and easy to manage as your project grows. Whether working on small projects or large applications, Git can help you streamline your database management processes and keep everything in sync across environments.

CHAPTER 18

SECURITY AND ACCESS CONTROL IN GIT AND GITHUB

Git and GitHub are powerful tools for version control and collaboration, but with great power comes the responsibility of ensuring your code and repositories remain secure. In this chapter, we will explore how to manage **secure access** to repositories using **SSH keys** and **HTTPS**, discuss the **privacy settings** of GitHub repositories (public vs private), understand **access control and permissions** in GitHub, and learn how to **set up and manage teams and collaborators** on GitHub for effective security and collaboration management.

Managing SSH Keys and HTTPS for Secure Access

Git provides two main methods for accessing repositories securely: **SSH keys** and **HTTPS**. Both methods provide a secure connection, but they have different configurations and use cases.

1. Using SSH Keys for Secure Access

SSH (Secure Shell) keys are the most common method for securely connecting to GitHub repositories. SSH keys allow you to authenticate with GitHub without needing to enter your username and password every time you interact with the repository.

- **Advantages of SSH**:
  - **Passwordless authentication**: Once set up, SSH keys allow you to authenticate without entering credentials.
  - **Security**: SSH keys are more secure than HTTPS because they rely on cryptographic pairs (private/public keys) instead of passwords.
  - **Convenient for frequent use**: Ideal for users who push, pull, or clone repositories frequently.
- **Setting Up SSH Keys**:
  1. **Generate an SSH Key Pair**: Run the following command in your terminal:

     ```bash
     ssh-keygen -t rsa -b 4096 -C "your_email@example.com"
     ```

     This will generate a public and private key pair. By default, the keys will be stored in `~/.ssh/id_rsa` (for Linux/Mac) or `C:\Users\<Username>\.ssh\id_rsa` (for Windows).

  2. **Add the SSH Key to GitHub**:

1. the public key to your clipboard:

```bash
```

```bash
cat ~/.ssh/id_rsa.pub
```

2. Log in to GitHub, go to **Settings → SSH and GPG keys → New SSH key**.
3. Paste the public key into the "Key" field, give it a title, and click **Add SSH key**.

3. **Test Your SSH Connection**: After adding the SSH key to GitHub, test the connection by running:

```bash
```

```bash
ssh -T git@github.com
```

2. Using HTTPS for Secure Access

HTTPS is an alternative to SSH for securely accessing GitHub repositories. While it requires you to enter your username and password (or a personal access token) every time you push or pull from the repository, it is a simpler option for users who don't want to manage SSH keys.

- **Advantages of HTTPS**:
  - **Simplicity**: Easy to set up, especially for users who are new to Git.

- o **No need to manage SSH keys**: If you don't want to deal with key generation and management, HTTPS is an easier method.
- **Authentication with Personal Access Tokens (PAT)**: In recent years, GitHub has replaced password authentication with **Personal Access Tokens (PATs)** for HTTPS access to increase security. Instead of entering your GitHub password, you'll enter a PAT.
  - o To create a PAT, go to **GitHub Settings → Developer settings → Personal access tokens**, then click **Generate new token**. Select the appropriate scopes and save the token.
  - o Use the token in place of your password when prompted for authentication during `git push` or `git pull`.

GitHub Repository Privacy: Public vs Private Repositories

GitHub allows users to control the visibility of their repositories, ensuring that sensitive or proprietary code can be kept private, while public projects can be shared with the wider community.

1. Public Repositories

Public repositories are open to anyone on the internet. They are ideal for open-source projects, collaborative work, and code that you want to share with the community.

- **Advantages of Public Repositories**:
  - **Visibility**: Open-source projects benefit from being public, allowing other developers to contribute and learn from the code.
  - **Collaboration**: Public repositories are easier to collaborate on since anyone can fork, clone, and open pull requests.

2. Private Repositories

Private repositories are only accessible to users with explicit permission. They are perfect for personal projects, internal codebases, or proprietary software that should not be shared with the public.

- **Advantages of Private Repositories**:
  - **Confidentiality**: Sensitive or proprietary code is kept private, reducing the risk of unauthorized access.
  - **Controlled Access**: Only invited collaborators can access the code, providing granular control over who can see and contribute to the project.
- **Setting Repository Privacy**:
  - **Creating a New Repository**: When creating a new repository, you can choose whether it's public or private.

o **Changing an Existing Repository's Privacy**: You can toggle the visibility of a repository from public to private or vice versa via the **Settings** tab in your repository.

Understanding Access Control and Permissions in GitHub

GitHub provides a detailed system for managing who has access to your repositories and what actions they can perform. This is important for maintaining security, particularly in teams or organizations.

1. User Roles and Permissions

GitHub allows you to set different levels of access for users based on their role within the repository. The main roles are:

- **Owner**: Full control over the repository. Owners can add or remove collaborators, change settings, and manage repository visibility.
- **Collaborator**: Users who have explicit access to a repository. They can push and pull code but cannot manage repository settings.
- **Contributor**: A general role for users who can make contributions but require pull requests to merge their changes.
- **Viewer**: In private repositories, viewers can see the contents but cannot make changes.

186

2. Managing Access Control in Teams and Organizations

If you are working in a **GitHub organization**, you can manage access to multiple repositories at once by organizing users into teams.

- **Teams**: Teams allow you to group users based on their roles or departments within the organization. Teams can be assigned access to specific repositories.
- **Repository Permissions**: You can assign **read**, **write**, or **admin** permissions to teams for each repository within the organization.
  - **Read**: Can view and clone the repository, but cannot push changes.
  - **Write**: Can view, clone, and push changes to the repository.
  - **Admin**: Can manage the repository's settings, collaborators, and access permissions.

3. Granting and Revoking Access

You can add collaborators to a repository via the **Settings** → **Manage access** tab. To add a collaborator:

1. Click **Invite a collaborator**.
2. Enter their GitHub username and select their role.
3. Send the invitation, and once they accept, they'll have access to the repository.

You can revoke access at any time by removing collaborators from the **Manage access** tab.

Setting Up and Managing Teams and Collaborators on GitHub

GitHub allows you to create teams within organizations, which can be assigned access permissions to repositories. Teams help streamline collaboration, especially for larger organizations.

1. Creating a Team in GitHub

To create a team:

1. Navigate to your **GitHub organization**.
2. Go to **Teams → New team**.
3. Give the team a name and description.
4. Assign repositories and set permissions (read, write, or admin).

2. Adding Collaborators to a Team

You can add collaborators to a team by:

1. Going to the **team page** within the organization.
2. Clicking **Add members** and entering their GitHub usernames.

3. Managing Team Permissions

You can fine-tune team permissions based on their role in the organization. For example, some teams may have read-only access to certain repositories, while others may be able to contribute code and manage issues.

4. Auditing Repository Access

You can monitor who has access to a repository and review their permissions under the **Settings** → **Manage access** tab. This ensures that only the right people have the necessary permissions to collaborate.

Conclusion

In this chapter, we explored how to secure access to your repositories using **SSH keys** and **HTTPS**. We also covered **repository privacy**, explaining the differences between **public** and **private repositories**, and understanding how **access control and permissions** work in GitHub. Additionally, we discussed how to set up and manage **teams** and **collaborators**, as well as the importance of maintaining **secure access** to your repositories, especially in a collaborative or organizational environment. By implementing these security and access control practices, you can ensure that your repositories remain secure, and that only the appropriate users have access to your code.

CHAPTER 19

USING GIT IN ENTERPRISE ENVIRONMENTS

Git is a powerful version control tool that can be seamlessly integrated into enterprise environments, where large teams and complex workflows demand efficient, scalable solutions. In this chapter, we'll explore how Git is used in **large enterprise systems**, the best practices for **implementing Git in a corporate environment**, how to **manage Git repositories in organizations**, and the **best practices for Git in large teams**.

Git in Large Enterprise Systems

In large enterprises, the software development process involves multiple teams working on various features, bug fixes, and other improvements across different environments. Managing version control in such systems requires careful planning and efficient management to ensure smooth collaboration, code quality, and scalability.

1. Challenges of Git in Large Enterprises

While Git is an excellent tool for version control, it introduces certain challenges in an enterprise environment:

- **Repository Size**: Large enterprises may have repositories with millions of lines of code and a massive history, which can impact performance.
- **Collaboration**: Multiple teams working on the same codebase require a well-organized branching strategy and clear communication to avoid merge conflicts.
- **Security**: Ensuring that sensitive data and code are protected from unauthorized access is paramount in an enterprise environment.
- **Continuous Integration and Delivery**: Enterprises need automated systems to ensure that new code changes don't break the application and are deployed effectively.

2. Scaling Git for Enterprise Needs

For large-scale projects and teams, Git can be scaled effectively by using additional tools and services like GitHub Enterprise, GitLab, Bitbucket, or self-hosted Git services. These tools provide features like advanced access controls, detailed audit logs, and better handling of large repositories.

- **Distributed Repositories**: Git's distributed nature allows each developer to work independently on their local of the repository, making it well-suited for large teams across different locations.
- **Branching Strategies**: Implementing robust branching strategies, such as **Git Flow** or **GitHub Flow**, helps

manage multiple features and releases efficiently in enterprise systems.

Implementing Git in a Corporate Environment

Introducing Git into a corporate environment involves understanding the needs of the organization and aligning Git's features with those needs. The implementation process should be smooth and strategic to ensure that the entire team adopts Git effectively.

1. Choosing the Right Git Service for Your Organization

The first step in implementing Git in a corporate environment is choosing a Git hosting platform that best fits the needs of the organization. Some popular options include:

- **GitHub Enterprise**: Offers enhanced collaboration features, security controls, and enterprise-level scalability.
- **GitLab**: Provides robust CI/CD features, issue tracking, and project management tools.
- **Bitbucket**: Suitable for teams using Atlassian tools, with built-in integration for Jira and Confluence.
- **Self-hosted Git Servers**: Some organizations may prefer to host their own Git servers to maintain complete control over their repositories and security.

2. Training and Onboarding Teams

Before migrating to Git, provide training sessions to help your team get familiar with Git's features and workflows. Create onboarding materials or workshops for new users that cover essential Git concepts, such as:

- Basic Git commands (clone, commit, push, pull)
- Branching strategies
- Conflict resolution
- Git workflows (e.g., Git Flow, GitHub Flow)

3. Integrating Git with Corporate Tools

Git can be integrated with other corporate tools to streamline workflows and improve productivity. For example:

- **CI/CD**: Tools like **Jenkins**, **CircleCI**, or **GitHub Actions** can be integrated with Git to automate the build and testing processes.
- **Project Management Tools**: Integrate Git with project management tools like **Jira** or **Trello** to track the progress of issues and user stories.
- **Code Review Tools**: Use GitHub Pull Requests, GitLab Merge Requests, or Bitbucket's Pull Requests for efficient code reviews.

4. Establishing Access Controls and Security

Access control is critical in an enterprise environment to ensure sensitive data and code are only accessible by authorized users. Git services like GitHub Enterprise and GitLab allow administrators to configure detailed permissions and access levels for different users and teams:

- **User Roles**: Define roles like admin, collaborator, and viewer with varying levels of access.
- **Branch Protections**: Set branch protection rules to prevent unauthorized changes to critical branches like `main` or `production`.
- **Security Audits**: Use GitHub's audit logs or GitLab's access logs to track user activities and identify any potential security breaches.

Managing Git Repositories in Organizations

Managing Git repositories in large organizations involves maintaining an organized structure, ensuring consistent workflows, and managing access permissions across teams.

1. Organizing Repositories

In large enterprises, it's important to define the structure of your Git repositories:

- **Monorepos** vs. **Multirepos**: In a monorepo setup, all codebases are stored in a single repository, while in a multirepo setup, each project or module has its own repository. The choice depends on the organization's structure and collaboration needs.

- **Repository Naming Conventions**: Establish a clear naming convention for repositories to make it easier for teams to navigate and understand the purpose of each repository (e.g., `product-name-backend`, `product-name-frontend`, `shared-library`).

2. Managing Large Repositories

Large repositories can become unwieldy and slow to clone, fetch, and manage. To mitigate performance issues:

- **Use Git LFS (Large File Storage)**: For repositories containing large binary files (e.g., images, videos, or datasets), use Git LFS to store these files outside of the Git history and keep the repository lightweight.

- **Shallow Clones**: To speed up cloning, use shallow clones (`git clone --depth 1`) to only fetch the latest commit and reduce the size of the repository.

3. Continuous Integration (CI) for Large Repositories

In large enterprise systems, it's essential to have automated testing and deployment pipelines to ensure code changes do not break the system. Integrating CI/CD tools with Git enables automated builds, tests, and deployments, streamlining the development process:

- **Automated Testing**: Set up automated testing to run on every commit or pull request to verify that new code doesn't introduce regressions.
- **Deployment Pipelines**: Use Git hooks and CI/CD tools to automatically deploy code changes to staging or production after passing tests.

4. Archiving Old Repositories

Over time, certain repositories may become obsolete or no longer in active development. It's good practice to archive or remove these repositories to avoid clutter and reduce maintenance overhead.

Best Practices for Git in Large Teams and Enterprises

Using Git effectively in large teams and enterprise environments requires adopting best practices to ensure smooth collaboration, maintain code quality, and avoid common pitfalls.

1. Implement a Branching Strategy

A well-defined branching strategy is crucial for managing multiple development streams, especially in larger teams. Popular strategies include:

- **Git Flow**: Defines separate branches for development, features, releases, and hotfixes. Suitable for projects with formal release cycles.
- **GitHub Flow**: A simpler strategy where all work is done in feature branches, and changes are merged directly into `main` via pull requests.
- **Trunk-Based Development**: Developers work directly in `main` or a single branch and make small, frequent commits.

2. Enforce Code Reviews

In large teams, code reviews are essential to maintain code quality and consistency. Use GitHub's Pull Requests (PRs) or GitLab Merge Requests (MRs) to facilitate reviews:

- **Require Approvals**: Set branch protection rules to require one or more approvals before merging a PR.
- **Automated Reviews**: Use tools like **SonarQube** or **CodeClimate** to automate code quality checks as part of the CI process.

3. Use Tags for Versioning

Use Git tags to mark stable releases or important milestones. Tags provide a way to refer to specific points in the repository's history, making it easier to track versions and roll back if necessary.

- **Semantic Versioning**: Use a versioning scheme like `v1.0.0`, `v1.1.0`, or `v2.0.0` to track changes and release cycles.

4. Protect Critical Branches

Prevent unauthorized changes to important branches like `main`, `production`, or `staging`. Use **branch protection rules** to:

- Require status checks to pass before merging.
- Require reviews from multiple team members.
- Prevent force-pushing to the branch.

5. Document Your Git Workflow

Clear documentation on how Git should be used within your team or organization is critical. This should include:

- Branching strategy
- Commit message conventions
- Pull request workflow
- Code review guidelines

- Git tagging policies

Conclusion

In this chapter, we explored how Git can be effectively used in large enterprise environments. We discussed the challenges and solutions for implementing Git in a corporate setting, managing repositories at scale, and applying best practices for collaboration, version control, and deployment. By adopting robust workflows, using Git efficiently, and implementing tools for CI/CD, enterprises can manage their software development processes more effectively and ensure secure, high-quality code delivery.

CHAPTER 20

TROUBLESHOOTING GIT ISSUES

Git is an incredibly powerful tool for version control, but like any tool, it comes with its share of challenges. Errors, conflicts, and mistakes are a part of working with Git, especially in complex projects. The good news is that many common Git issues can be easily fixed, and in some cases, Git provides powerful tools to recover from mistakes. In this chapter, we'll cover **common Git errors and how to fix them, how to recover lost commits and branches, using `git reflog` to recover from mistakes**, and **dealing with broken repositories and corrupt files**.

Common Git Errors and How to Fix Them

Understanding common Git errors and how to troubleshoot them is a crucial skill for developers. Below are some of the most frequent Git errors you might encounter and how to resolve them.

1. Error: "Merge Conflict"

A merge conflict occurs when Git cannot automatically merge changes from two different branches. This typically happens when two branches modify the same line of code or file.

- **How to Fix**:

200

1. Git will mark the conflicting areas in the file with conflict markers like <<<<<<<, =======, and >>>>>>>.

2. Open the conflicting files and resolve the conflicts manually by choosing which changes to keep.

3. After resolving the conflicts, stage the files using:

```bash
```

```bash
git add <file-name>
```

4. Complete the merge by committing the changes:

```bash
```

```bash
git commit
```

2. Error: "Your branch is behind 'origin/main' by X commits"

This error occurs when your local branch is out of sync with the remote branch, usually because someone else has pushed new commits to the remote repository since your last pull.

- **How to Fix**:
    1. First, pull the changes from the remote repository:

```bash
```

```
git pull origin main
```

2. If there are conflicts, resolve them as mentioned above.

3. After pulling and resolving conflicts, push your changes back to the remote:

```bash
git push origin main
```

3. Error: "fatal: refusing to merge unrelated histories"

This error occurs when you try to merge two Git repositories or branches that have no common ancestor. This typically happens when you try to merge a branch or repo that was initialized independently.

- **How to Fix**: To merge two unrelated histories, use the --allow-unrelated-histories flag:

```bash
git merge <branch-name> --allow-unrelated-histories
```

This error occurs when Git cannot authenticate you using SSH keys. This typically happens when your SSH key isn't set up properly or is missing from GitHub or another Git host.

- **How to Fix**:
    1. Check if your SSH key is added to your GitHub account by running:

       ```bash
       bash

       ssh -T git@github.com
       ```

    2. If not, follow the instructions for setting up and adding an SSH key on GitHub or your Git hosting platform.
    3. Add your SSH key to GitHub by going to **Settings → SSH and GPG keys → New SSH key**.

5. Error: "fatal: not a git repository (or any of the parent directories)"

This error means you are trying to run a Git command outside of a Git repository (i.e., the current directory is not initialized as a Git repository).

- **How to Fix**:
    1. Navigate to the correct directory that contains the Git repository.
    2. Verify if you are in a Git repository by running:

    ```bash
    git status
    ```

    3. If the directory is not a Git repository, initialize it with:

    ```bash
    git init
    ```

How to Recover Lost Commits and Branches

At times, you may inadvertently lose commits or even entire branches, either through an incorrect `git reset` or by accidentally deleting a branch. Fortunately, Git provides powerful tools to recover lost commits and branches.

1. Recovering Lost Commits

If you lost commits due to a reset, checkout, or rebase, Git might still have references to those commits in its reflog.

- **How to Recover Lost Commits**:

  1. Use `git reflog` to find the commit you want to recover:

     bash

     ```
     git reflog
     ```

     This will show a history of all the recent actions in your Git repository, including commits, checkouts, resets, and rebase actions.

  2. Identify the commit hash of the lost commit from the reflog.

  3. Use `git checkout` or `git reset` to move your HEAD to the desired commit:

     bash

     ```
     git checkout <commit-hash>
     ```

2. Recovering a Deleted Branch

If you accidentally delete a branch, you can recover it by looking at the reflog.

- **How to Recover a Deleted Branch**:

  1. Use `git reflog` to find the commit where the branch was last checked out.

205

2. Once you identify the commit, you can create a new branch from it:

```bash
git checkout -b <branch-name> <commit-hash>
```

Using `git reflog` to Recover from Mistakes

`git reflog` is a powerful tool that records every movement of the HEAD pointer. This means you can use it to recover from mistakes, such as losing a commit or accidentally resetting your branch.

1. What is `git reflog`?

`git reflog` keeps track of where your HEAD and branch references have been. It stores a history of all operations, including commits, checkouts, merges, and rebase operations.

2. How to Use `git reflog`

- Run `git reflog` to view the history of your Git repository:

```bash
```

```
git reflog
```

The output will display something like this:

```
pgsql
```

```
e94a8e9 HEAD@{0}: commit: Added new feature
7ac9d4e  HEAD@{1}:  checkout:  moving  from
feature-branch to main
1d2f3b5 HEAD@{2}: reset: moving to HEAD~1
```

- Each entry includes a reference number (HEAD@{n}), where n is the number of steps back in the reflog. You can use these references to recover previous states.

3. Recovering a Commit Using `git reflog`

Once you've found the commit in the reflog that you want to restore, you can use `git checkout` or `git reset` to revert to that commit.

- **Using `git checkout`:**

```
bash
```

```
git checkout HEAD@{2}
```

- **Using `git reset`** (if you want to make the change permanent in your current branch):

```bash
bash
```

```bash
git reset --hard HEAD@{2}
```

This allows you to move your branch pointer to a specific commit from the reflog.

Dealing with Broken Repositories and Corrupt Files

Occasionally, a Git repository can become corrupt due to various reasons, such as interruptions during commits or hardware failures. There are a few tools and techniques to fix a broken repository or recover from corrupted files.

1. Repairing a Broken Git Repository

If your repository is broken (e.g., due to a corrupt .git directory), you can try to repair it using the following methods:

- **Clone a fresh of the repository**: If your repository is hosted on a remote server (e.g., GitHub, GitLab), you can clone it again from the remote and move any local changes over.

  ```bash
  bash
  ```

```
git                                clone
https://github.com/username/repository.gi
t
```

- **Rebuild the Repository**: If your `.git` directory is corrupt, you can attempt to rebuild the repository by running the following commands:
    1. Back up the current repository.
    2. Remove the `.git` directory (this deletes your local history).
    3. Reinitialize Git:

    ```bash
    git init
    git remote add origin <repository-url>
    git fetch
    ```

2. Fixing Corrupt Files

If specific files in your repository are corrupted, you can use Git to checkout the last known good version of the file:

- **Checking out a Specific File**:

```bash
git checkout HEAD~1 -- path/to/corrupt-file
```

This will retrieve the file from the previous commit.

Conclusion

In this chapter, we discussed how to troubleshoot and fix common Git issues that developers face, including errors, lost commits and branches, and broken repositories. By leveraging tools like `git reflog`, using best practices for managing commits and branches, and understanding common Git errors, you can efficiently recover from mistakes and maintain a clean and functional Git workflow. With these troubleshooting techniques, you'll be better equipped to handle the challenges that come with using Git in large-scale projects and teams.

CHAPTER 21

WORKING WITH GIT FROM THE COMMAND LINE VS GUI TOOLS

Git is a versatile version control system, and it offers both **command-line** and **graphical user interface (GUI)** options for managing your repositories. Whether you're a beginner or an experienced developer, you might wonder which method to choose for interacting with Git. In this chapter, we'll compare **Git from the command line** and **GUI tools** like **GitHub Desktop, Sourcetree**, and **GitKraken**, discuss the **pros and cons** of using a GUI, and provide guidance on **when to use the command line** and **when to use GUI tools**.

The Git Command Line vs Graphical Tools (GitHub Desktop, Sourcetree, GitKraken)

1. The Git Command Line

The **Git command line interface (CLI)** is the most direct and powerful way to interact with Git. It involves typing Git commands directly into the terminal or command prompt, which provides full access to all Git features.

- **Popular Git Command Line Commands**:
    - o `git init`: Initialize a new Git repository.

o   `git clone`: Clone a remote repository.

o   `git add`: Add changes to the staging area.

o   `git commit`: Commit staged changes.

o   `git push`: Push changes to a remote repository.

o   `git pull`: Pull changes from a remote repository.

o   `git status`: Check the current status of the repository.

2. Graphical Tools for Git

GUI tools for Git provide a visual interface that allows you to interact with Git repositories using buttons, menus, and icons, rather than typing commands. Popular Git GUI tools include:

- **GitHub Desktop**: A GUI client designed by GitHub for users who prefer to work with Git without using the command line.
- **Sourcetree**: A free Git GUI tool by Atlassian that supports Git and Mercurial repositories. It's particularly useful for users who want a more detailed view of their repository's history and branching.
- **GitKraken**: A powerful Git GUI tool that provides a visual interface for managing repositories, creating branches, and resolving merge conflicts. It offers a more modern and visually appealing interface with advanced features for managing complex workflows.

3. Features Comparison

Feature	Command Line	GitHub Desktop	Sourcetree	GitKraken
Ease of Use	Requires knowledge of commands	Simple, user-friendly interface	Intermediate-level interface	Intuitive, visually appealing
Full Git Features	Full access to all Git features	Limited features compared to CLI	Full Git features with a GUI	Full Git features with advanced tools
Branching and Merging	Manual command input	Visualize branches with limited options	Advanced branching and merge visualization	Comprehensive branch and merge management
Conflict Resolution	Manual conflict resolution	Basic merge conflict management	Conflict resolution tools available	Advanced conflict resolution tools

Feature	Command Line	GitHub Desktop	Sourcetree	GitKraken
Customization and Flexibility	High (command flexibility)	Low (limited to GitHub features)	Medium (more options than GitHub Desktop)	High (visual and feature customization)
Learning Curve	Steep for beginners	Low for beginners	Medium	Low to Medium

Pros and Cons of Using Git with a GUI

Using Git through a graphical interface provides several advantages, but also has certain limitations. Below, we'll review the **pros and cons** of using a Git GUI.

Pros of Using a Git GUI:

1. **User-Friendly**: GUI tools are generally easier to use, especially for beginners who may find the command line intimidating. The graphical interface simplifies complex Git tasks like branching, merging, and viewing commit history.

2. **Visual Representation**: GUI tools provide a visual representation of your project's branches, commits, and

214

changes, making it easier to understand the state of the repository at any given point.

3. **Fewer Command Errors**: Since GUI tools automate most actions, they reduce the risk of errors caused by incorrect or forgotten commands.

4. **Conflict Resolution**: Many GUI tools provide an intuitive interface for resolving merge conflicts, with visual aids for comparing and merging conflicting changes.

5. **Integration with Services**: Tools like GitHub Desktop and Sourcetree often come integrated with popular Git hosting services (e.g., GitHub, Bitbucket), making it easier to perform actions like pull requests and pushing commits.

Cons of Using a Git GUI:

1. **Limited Flexibility**: While GUI tools cover most Git operations, they do not expose all Git features and options available in the command line. Advanced operations may require switching to the command line.

2. **Performance**: GUI tools can be slower than the command line, especially when working with large repositories or many branches.

3. **Less Control**: Some users prefer the control and precision that the command line offers. GUI tools tend to abstract away the finer details of Git operations.

4. **Over-Simplification**: Some users might find that GUI tools abstract too much of the Git workflow, making it harder to learn and understand Git deeply.

When to Use the Command Line and When to Use GUI Tools

While both command-line Git and GUI tools are powerful, choosing the right tool depends on the task at hand, your experience level, and your workflow.

When to Use the Command Line:

1. **Advanced Git Operations**:
   - If you need to execute advanced Git commands or fine-tune your version control workflow (e.g., rebasing, squashing commits, cherry-picking, and resolving complex merge conflicts), the command line is your best option.
   - The command line gives you full control and flexibility over your repository.

2. **Automation**:
   - If you want to automate certain tasks with scripts or integrate Git into CI/CD pipelines, you'll need to use the command line. Git commands can easily be scripted to perform operations in an automated fashion.

3. **Better Performance**:
  o The command line is faster than most GUI tools, especially when working with large repositories, numerous branches, or large amounts of data.

4. **Learning Git**:
  o If you want to understand Git deeply and learn all of its capabilities, working with the command line is essential. It teaches you the underlying mechanics of Git and gives you a more comprehensive view of how version control works.

5. **Complex Repository Management**:
  o In scenarios where you are managing large projects with intricate branching strategies (e.g., Git Flow or trunk-based development), the command line allows for precise control over the repository.

When to Use GUI Tools:

1. **Beginner Git Users**:
  o If you're just starting with Git and want to avoid the steep learning curve of the command line, a GUI tool like GitHub Desktop, Sourcetree, or GitKraken can be a great introduction. These tools allow you to perform basic Git operations without needing to memorize commands.

2. **Visualizing Repositories**:

    o   For tasks where you need to visualize the project's commit history, branches, and merges (e.g., understanding how different features are integrated or reviewing the history), GUI tools provide a clear, intuitive view of your repository.

3. **Simplified Git Workflows**:

    o   If you're working on smaller projects or don't need the full power of Git, a GUI tool can speed up your workflow. Operations like committing changes, pushing and pulling, and managing branches can be done quickly with a few clicks.

4. **Resolving Merge Conflicts**:

    o   GUI tools like GitKraken and Sourcetree offer easy-to-use interfaces for resolving merge conflicts, making it simpler to compare files side-by-side and decide which changes to keep.

5. **Integration with Git Hosting Services**:

    o   GUI tools like GitHub Desktop and Sourcetree are tightly integrated with Git hosting services, which makes tasks like creating pull requests, viewing issues, and pushing changes more straightforward. If you're working with services like GitHub or Bitbucket, a GUI tool might simplify those workflows.

Conclusion

In this chapter, we compared using Git through the **command line** and **graphical tools** like **GitHub Desktop**, **Sourcetree**, and **GitKraken**. Both methods have their strengths and weaknesses, and the best choice depends on the specific needs of the task and your experience level. The **command line** provides greater flexibility, control, and is preferred for advanced operations, while **GUI tools** offer an easier, more visual approach suitable for beginners or simpler tasks. Understanding when to use each method will help you become more efficient and comfortable in your Git workflow, whether you're managing small projects or working in large teams with complex repositories.

CHAPTER 22

INTEGRATING GIT WITH OTHER TOOLS

Git is a central part of many development workflows, and integrating it with other tools can significantly improve your productivity and streamline your processes. Whether you're working in an Integrated Development Environment (IDE), using project management tools, or developing containerized applications with Docker, Git can be seamlessly integrated into these systems. In this chapter, we'll explore how to **integrate Git with IDEs (VSCode, IntelliJ IDEA)**, how to **link Git with project management tools (Jira, Trello)**, and how to use **Git with Docker** for version control in containerized applications.

Git and IDE Integration (VSCode, IntelliJ IDEA, etc.)

Most modern Integrated Development Environments (IDEs) offer built-in support for Git, which can make version control tasks easier and more integrated with your development workflow. These integrations allow you to perform Git operations directly within the IDE, without switching to the command line.

1. Git Integration in VSCode

Visual Studio Code (VSCode) is a popular, lightweight code editor that provides integrated Git support, making it a great choice for developers who want a fast and efficient workflow with Git.

- **Git Features in VSCode**:
  - **Source Control View**: VSCode has a dedicated source control panel where you can view changes, commit code, create branches, and manage repositories.
  - **Inline Git Status**: VSCode shows the status of your repository (modified files, staged changes, etc.) directly in the file explorer and editor.
  - **Commit and Push**: You can easily commit changes, write commit messages, and push to remote repositories directly from the IDE.
  - **Branch Management**: Switch branches, create new branches, and view the current branch directly in the interface.
  - **GitLens Extension**: This extension enhances Git capabilities in VSCode by providing advanced features like blame annotations, commit history, and repository insights.
- **How to Use Git in VSCode**:
  1. Open your project in VSCode.

2. The Git panel will automatically show any repositories present in your workspace. If there is no repository initialized, you can initialize one by running `git init` in the terminal or directly from the VSCode interface.

3. Stage, commit, and push changes through the source control panel, where you can select files to stage, write commit messages, and sync with the remote repository.

2. Git Integration in IntelliJ IDEA

IntelliJ IDEA is a powerful IDE used primarily for Java development, but it also supports many other languages. It provides excellent Git integration for both beginners and advanced users.

- **Git Features in IntelliJ IDEA**:
  - **Version Control Panel**: IntelliJ has a dedicated version control panel where you can track and manage all Git operations like commits, branches, and remote interactions.
  - **Commit Tool Window**: A GUI tool to help you stage changes, write commit messages, and view the changes made to each file.

- o **Branch and Merge Management**: You can switch between branches, merge branches, and handle merge conflicts visually.

- o **Git Flow Support**: IntelliJ IDEA provides support for the Git Flow branching model, allowing you to manage features, releases, and hotfixes with ease.

- o **Interactive Rebase**: You can also perform interactive rebases to clean up your commit history, without needing to use the command line.

- **How to Use Git in IntelliJ IDEA**:
  1. Open your project in IntelliJ IDEA and connect to a Git repository (if not already connected).
  2. Use the **Git tool window** to manage commits, branches, and repositories.
  3. Use the **Commit** window to stage and commit files. You can also access the history of commits and manage branches from here.
  4. Push, pull, or fetch from the remote repository directly through the Git tool window.

Integrating Git with Project Management Tools (Jira, Trello, etc.)

Project management tools like **Jira** and **Trello** are essential for tracking tasks, bugs, and features. Integrating Git with these tools can help keep your development workflow aligned with project progress, provide better traceability, and automate updates between tools.

1. Git and Jira Integration

Jira, by Atlassian, is one of the most widely used project management tools for tracking issues, bugs, and project tasks. By integrating Git with Jira, you can automatically link Git commits and branches with Jira issues.

- **How Git Integrates with Jira**:
    - **Smart Commits**: Jira supports smart commits, which allow you to link Git commit messages directly to Jira issues. By including the issue key in your commit message, Jira can automatically track the commit and display it within the issue. Example commit message:

      ```sql
      git commit -m "PROJ-123 Fixed issue with user authentication"
      ```

      This commit will link the change to the **PROJ-123** issue in Jira.

    - **Branching**: You can create branches directly from Jira issues using branch templates that include the issue key (e.g., `feature/PROJ-123`), which makes it easier to track the task associated with the branch.

o **Automated Status Updates**: Using the Git integration, you can automatically transition Jira issue statuses based on commit actions (e.g., when a commit is made, the status can automatically change to "In Progress" or "Done").

- **Integrating Git with Jira**:
  1. Connect your Git repository to Jira by using a Git integration plugin (e.g., **Bitbucket, GitHub**, or **GitLab** integration).
  2. Enable smart commits by including Jira issue keys in your commit messages.
  3. Use the Jira interface to view commits, pull requests, and branches related to specific issues.

2. Git and Trello Integration

Trello is a flexible project management tool that helps teams organize tasks visually on boards and cards. Integrating Git with Trello provides a more seamless connection between the development process and project tracking.

- **How Git Integrates with Trello**:

- o **GitHub Power-Up for Trello**: Trello offers a GitHub Power-Up that lets you attach GitHub pull requests, branches, and commits to Trello cards. This allows your team to easily track development progress directly within Trello.
- o **Automated Card Updates**: When changes are made in Git (e.g., a commit is pushed), Trello cards can be automatically updated with relevant information like commit messages and pull request links.

- **Integrating Git with Trello**:
  1. Install the GitHub Power-Up in Trello from the Power-Up directory.
  2. Connect your GitHub account to Trello.
  3. Attach GitHub pull requests, commits, and issues to Trello cards to track progress.

Git and Docker: Version Control for Containerized Applications

Git is essential for managing application source code, while **Docker** is used for creating containerized environments for application deployment. Integrating Git with Docker allows you to version control both your code and Docker configuration files, ensuring that your development and production environments are consistent.

1. Using Git for Docker Configuration Files

Docker relies on configuration files like the `Dockerfile` (for building containers) and `docker-compose.yml` (for managing multi-container applications). These files can be stored in Git repositories to track changes, collaborate with other developers, and ensure consistency.

- **Managing Dockerfiles in Git**: The `Dockerfile` defines the steps for building a Docker image. Storing it in Git ensures that all team members use the same base image and instructions when building containers.

  ```
  Dockerfile
  ```

  ```
  # Example Dockerfile
  FROM node:14
  WORKDIR /app

    . .

  RUN npm install
  CMD ["npm", "start"]
  ```

- **Versioning Docker Compose Configurations**: If your application uses multiple containers (e.g., a backend service and a database), you can use `docker-compose.yml` to define how these containers interact. Versioning this file with Git helps maintain the configuration over time.

227

2. Using Git and Docker for CI/CD Pipelines

You can integrate Git and Docker in your CI/CD pipelines to automate the process of building and deploying Docker images. When code is pushed to Git, Docker can automatically build and deploy the updated image to a staging or production environment.

- **Example CI/CD Pipeline**: Using **GitHub Actions**, you can automate Docker builds and deployments:

```yaml
name: Build and Deploy Docker Image

on:
  push:
    branches:
      - main

jobs:
  build:
    runs-on: ubuntu-latest
    steps:
      - name: Checkout repository
        uses: actions/checkout@v2

      - name: Set up Docker Buildx
        uses:            docker/setup-buildx-action@v1
```

```
    - name: Cache Docker layers
      uses: actions/cache@v2
      with:
        path: /tmp/.buildx-cache
        key: ${{ runner.os }}-buildx-${{
github.sha }}
        restore-keys: |
          ${{ runner.os }}-buildx-

    - name: Build and push Docker image
      uses: docker/build-push-action@v2
      with:
        context: .
        push: true
        tags:                          ${{
secrets.DOCKER_USERNAME }}/my-app:latest
```

This GitHub Actions workflow automatically builds and pushes a Docker image to Docker Hub whenever code is pushed to the `main` branch.

Conclusion

In this chapter, we explored how to **integrate Git with other tools**, including **IDEs** like **VSCode** and **IntelliJ IDEA**, **project management tools** like **Jira** and **Trello**, and **Docker** for containerized application management. By integrating Git with

229

these tools, you can improve collaboration, automate workflows, and ensure consistency across your development environments. Whether you're managing code with an IDE, tracking tasks with a project management tool, or deploying containerized applications with Docker, Git serves as the backbone that ties all these tools together.

CHAPTER 23

VERSION CONTROL BEYOND GIT: OTHER SYSTEMS

While **Git** is the most popular version control system (VCS) today, it's not the only option available. There are other VCS options like **SVN** (Subversion) and **Mercurial** that have been widely used in the past and continue to be employed in specific use cases. Understanding how these version control systems compare to Git, and when to choose one over the other, is crucial for developers and teams. In this chapter, we'll explore **SVN**, **Mercurial**, and other version control systems, compare them to Git, and discuss **when to choose Git over other VCS** and vice versa.

Overview of Other Version Control Systems: SVN, Mercurial

1. SVN (Subversion)

SVN is a centralized version control system (CVCS) that was widely used before Git became the dominant version control system. In SVN, the repository is stored on a central server, and developers must check out a working of the code from that server to make changes. After making changes, they commit the changes back to the central repository.

- **Key Features of SVN**:
  - o **Centralized Repository**: All code changes are stored in a central repository, and every developer checks out a of the project from that server.
  - o **Simpler for Small Teams**: SVN is easier to set up for small teams and projects, and it's easier to manage than decentralized systems like Git.
  - o **Supports Binary Files**: SVN works well with binary files since it's optimized for versioning large files and large datasets.
  - o **Strong Support for Branching and Tagging**: SVN supports branching and tagging, but the process is not as streamlined or flexible as in Git.
- **SVN Workflow**:
  1. Checkout: Retrieve the working from the central server.
  2. Modify: Make changes locally.
  3. Commit: Push your changes back to the central repository.

2. Mercurial

Mercurial is a distributed version control system similar to Git, with the main difference being its design philosophy and user experience. Mercurial is known for being easy to use and fast, offering some of the same advantages of Git, such as working offline and tracking project history.

- **Key Features of Mercurial**:
  - **Distributed Version Control**: Like Git, Mercurial allows each developer to have a full of the repository and history.
  - **Simplicity**: Mercurial is designed to be easier to use than Git, with simpler commands and workflows. The user interface is less complex, and it's easier for beginners to pick up.
  - **Performance**: Mercurial is known for being fast, especially when handling large repositories.
  - **Repository Size**: Mercurial typically handles repositories with larger histories better than Git in terms of performance and speed.
- **Mercurial Workflow**:
  1. Clone: Clone the entire repository and history to your local machine.
  2. Modify: Make changes to your local working .
  3. Commit: Commit changes locally.
  4. Push: Push your changes to the remote repository.

How Git Compares to These Systems

1. Centralized vs Distributed Version Control

One of the biggest differences between **Git** and **SVN** is that Git is a **distributed version control system (DVCS)**, while SVN is a **centralized version control system (CVCS)**.

- **Centralized Version Control (SVN)**:
  - o In SVN, the repository is stored on a central server, and every developer must be connected to that server to make changes. If the central repository is down or unreachable, developers cannot commit changes, making it less reliable for working offline.
  - o In SVN, branching and merging are more difficult, as SVN is optimized for linear workflows (main trunk development).
- **Distributed Version Control (Git and Mercurial)**:
  - o Both Git and Mercurial are **distributed**, meaning every developer has a full of the repository, including its history. This allows for offline work, as developers can commit, branch, and merge without needing to connect to a central server.
  - o Git and Mercurial both excel at branching and merging, which are streamlined and flexible. In contrast, SVN's branching model is less efficient and more prone to issues.

2. Branching and Merging

- **SVN**: Branching and merging in SVN can be cumbersome and error-prone. Merges often require manual intervention and can result in conflicts that are difficult to resolve.

- **Mercurial**: Branching and merging are much more efficient in Mercurial compared to SVN. It is also a distributed system, so it supports offline work and local repositories.

- **Git**: Git has a very advanced and flexible branching and merging model. It's easy to create, switch between, and merge branches, making Git ideal for feature-driven development and parallel workflows. Git's merging capabilities, especially with the `rebase` command, are extremely powerful.

3. Performance

- **SVN**: SVN performs well with smaller repositories or projects that don't require a lot of branching. However, performance can degrade with large repositories or projects with lots of branches.

- **Mercurial**: Mercurial generally has better performance than SVN when dealing with large repositories. Its design allows it to handle large projects with a large number of files more efficiently than SVN.

- **Git**: Git outperforms both SVN and Mercurial in terms of performance, especially with large codebases. Git's ability to handle large projects is unmatched, particularly in distributed environments.

4. Learning Curve

- **SVN**: SVN is generally easier for beginners to pick up since it has a simpler model of version control (centralized). You don't need to worry about concepts like branching and merging as much.
- **Mercurial**: Mercurial is simpler and less complex than Git, which can make it a good choice for teams looking for a more user-friendly system while still benefiting from the distributed version control model.
- **Git**: Git has a steeper learning curve due to its flexibility and more advanced features. However, it is well worth learning for its powerful branching and merging capabilities, speed, and widespread adoption.

When to Choose Git Over Other VCS and Vice Versa

When to Choose Git:

1. **For Distributed Version Control**: If you need a distributed system that allows developers to work offline, Git is the best option. With Git, you can work on branches, commits, and merges locally and sync with a central repository when needed.
2. **For Large Teams or Complex Projects**: Git is ideal for larger teams and projects with complex branching and merging needs. It provides flexibility in workflows, such

as Git Flow, and works well with automated CI/CD pipelines.

3. **When You Need Speed and Flexibility**: Git is optimized for handling large repositories with ease, providing fast performance, and offering flexibility in branching and merging.

4. **When Collaborating with Open Source**: Git is the dominant version control system used in open-source projects. If you are contributing to open-source or working on collaborative projects, Git is the system you will encounter most often.

When to Choose SVN:

1. **For Small Teams or Simple Workflows**: If you have a small project or a simple development workflow (where you don't need a lot of branching), SVN can be an easier solution to set up and maintain.

2. **When You Need a Centralized System**: If your team prefers working with a centralized version control system and requires the benefits of a single source of truth, SVN is a good choice.

3. **For Legacy Projects**: Some older enterprise systems use SVN. If you're working on or maintaining legacy codebases that already use SVN, it may be best to stick with SVN unless a migration to Git is absolutely necessary.

When to Choose Mercurial:

1. **For Simple, Fast Distributed Version Control**: If you need a distributed version control system but want something simpler than Git, Mercurial is a good choice. It has an easier learning curve than Git and offers many of the same features.

2. **When Performance with Large Repositories is Important**: Mercurial offers good performance when dealing with large repositories and is a better choice for projects that are too complex for SVN but don't need the advanced features of Git.

3. **For Smaller Teams**: Mercurial's interface is simpler and can be a better fit for small teams or individual developers who don't need the full complexity of Git.

Conclusion

In this chapter, we discussed several key version control systems, including **SVN**, **Mercurial**, and **Git**, and explored how Git compares to these other systems in terms of **centralized vs distributed version control**, **branching and merging**, **performance**, and **ease of use**.

While **Git** is generally the best choice for modern, large-scale projects and distributed teams due to its flexibility, speed, and powerful features, **SVN** may still be suitable for smaller, centralized systems with simpler workflows. **Mercurial** strikes a balance between the two, offering a distributed model with a simpler interface than Git.

Ultimately, the choice between Git and other version control systems depends on the scale and complexity of your project, the workflows of your team, and the tools that best support your development process.

CHAPTER 24

UNDERSTANDING GIT WORKFLOWS

A **Git workflow** defines the process and rules by which developers interact with a Git repository to manage changes. Having a well-defined Git workflow is crucial in both small and large teams, ensuring that everyone follows the same processes for feature development, code review, release management, and collaboration. In this chapter, we'll discuss popular Git workflows like **GitHub Flow** and **Git Flow**, explore branching strategies such as **feature branching**, **trunk-based development**, and **GitOps**, and offer guidance on **implementing Git workflows in a team**.

GitHub Flow vs Git Flow: Choosing the Right Workflow

1. GitHub Flow

GitHub Flow is a simple, lightweight workflow designed for continuous delivery and frequent releases. It is commonly used for teams that deploy to production frequently and prefer to keep the process as streamlined as possible.

- **Key Features of GitHub Flow:**

o **Main Branch**: GitHub Flow assumes that the `main` branch is always in a deployable state. Code is pushed to `main` via pull requests.

o **Feature Branches**: Developers create feature branches off the `main` branch to develop new features, fix bugs, or implement changes. Once a feature is complete, it is merged into `main` via a pull request.

o **Pull Requests (PRs)**: Changes are reviewed and discussed before being merged into the main branch. This is ideal for smaller teams or teams practicing continuous delivery.

o **No Release Branches**: GitHub Flow does not require dedicated release branches. Instead, `main` is always the latest stable version of the code.

- **Typical GitHub Flow Workflow**:

  1. Checkout from `main` and create a new feature branch.

  2. Make commits to the feature branch.

  3. Open a pull request to merge the feature branch into `main`.

  4. After code review, merge the feature branch into `main`.

  5. Deploy from `main` to production.

- **When to Use GitHub Flow**:

241

- o Ideal for teams with small-to-medium-sized projects that release frequently and want a simple, lightweight workflow.
- o Perfect for projects that deploy directly from the `main` branch and rely on continuous integration/deployment (CI/CD).
- o Suitable for teams that work with pull requests for code review.

2. Git Flow

Git Flow is a more structured workflow designed for teams that follow a more traditional release cycle. It is ideal for larger projects with planned release versions and hotfixes. Git Flow is well-suited for teams that want to manage multiple stages of development (e.g., development, staging, production) and need a more formal branching strategy.

- • **Key Features of Git Flow**:
  - o **Main Branch**: Like GitHub Flow, Git Flow uses the `main` branch, but it treats `main` as the stable production branch.
  - o **Develop Branch**: Git Flow uses a `develop` branch, which is used for ongoing development. New features are merged into `develop` first.

- o **Feature Branches**: Feature branches are created from `develop`. Once a feature is complete, it's merged back into `develop`.
- o **Release Branches**: A release branch is created from `develop` when preparing for a release. This allows for final bug fixes and versioning before being merged into `main` and `develop`.
- o **Hotfix Branches**: Hotfix branches are created from `main` to fix critical issues in production. After the hotfix is completed, it is merged into both `main` and `develop`.

- **Typical Git Flow Workflow**:
  1. Create a new feature branch from `develop`.
  2. Work on the feature and commit changes to the feature branch.
  3. When the feature is complete, merge it back into `develop`.
  4. When preparing for a release, create a `release` branch from `develop`.
  5. After finalizing the release, merge the `release` branch into `main` and `develop`.
  6. If needed, create a `hotfix` branch from `main` to address production issues.

- **When to Use Git Flow**:
  - o Ideal for teams working with well-defined release cycles or scheduled software releases.

- o Best suited for projects that require detailed versioning and need multiple environments (e.g., staging, production).
- o Useful for larger teams that need clear branching strategies for different types of changes (features, releases, hotfixes).

Feature Branching, Trunk-Based Development, and GitOps

1. Feature Branching

Feature branching is a common Git workflow where each feature or bug fix is developed in its own branch. The main idea is to keep the `main` branch stable while developers work on isolated branches.

- **Key Benefits of Feature Branching**:
  - o **Isolation**: Each feature or bug fix is worked on independently, preventing interruptions to the main branch.
  - o **Collaboration**: Multiple developers can work on different features simultaneously without interfering with each other's work.
  - o **Code Reviews**: Feature branches provide clear boundaries for reviewing code before merging it into `main`.
- **When to Use Feature Branching**:

244

- o Ideal for teams working on individual features or fixes that can be developed independently.
- o Suitable for teams that need to maintain a stable `main` branch while still developing multiple features at once.

2. Trunk-Based Development

Trunk-based development is a development strategy where developers work directly on the `main` branch (referred to as "trunk") and make small, frequent commits. Rather than maintaining long-lived feature branches, developers create small, incremental changes and continuously integrate their work into the `main` branch.

- **Key Benefits of Trunk-Based Development**:
  - o **Fast Integration**: Developers integrate their changes regularly, reducing the risk of large conflicts or integration issues later in the process.
  - o **Continuous Delivery**: Trunk-based development supports continuous delivery, where the code is always in a deployable state.
  - o **Simplified Workflow**: With fewer long-lived feature branches, the workflow becomes simpler and more streamlined.
- **When to Use Trunk-Based Development**:

o Ideal for teams practicing continuous integration and delivery (CI/CD).

o Suitable for smaller teams or projects that require frequent integration and quick iterations.

3. GitOps

GitOps is a modern approach to managing infrastructure and application deployments using Git as the source of truth. In a GitOps workflow, all infrastructure and application configurations are stored in Git repositories, and deployments are automated based on changes in these repositories.

- **Key Benefits of GitOps**:
  - o **Declarative Configurations**: GitOps uses declarative configuration files to manage deployments, meaning the desired state of infrastructure and applications is defined in Git.
  - o **Automated Deployments**: Changes to Git repositories trigger automated deployment pipelines, making the process of updating applications and infrastructure seamless and repeatable.
  - o **Version Control for Infrastructure**: Infrastructure changes are versioned in Git, providing a clear history of changes to the environment.

- **When to Use GitOps**:
  - o Ideal for teams practicing continuous delivery and looking for automated and repeatable deployment processes.
  - o Suitable for infrastructure management, where all configurations and changes are versioned and managed in Git.

Implementing Git Workflows in a Team

Choosing the right Git workflow and implementing it effectively in a team is critical for maintaining a smooth development process. Here are some steps for implementing Git workflows in a team:

1. Establish Clear Branching and Merging Rules

Define which Git workflow (e.g., GitHub Flow, Git Flow, feature branching) best suits the team's needs, and establish clear rules for how branches should be named, when to create branches, and how merges should be handled.

- **Branch Naming Conventions**: Decide on a consistent naming scheme for branches (e.g., `feature/feature-name`, `bugfix/issue-id`, `hotfix/urgent-fix`).

- **Merge Strategies**: Establish rules for how and when to merge branches. For example, you may want to use pull requests for code review before merging into `main`.

2. Set Up Automated Workflows

Implement automated processes for continuous integration and continuous delivery (CI/CD) using Git workflows. Set up hooks, triggers, or GitHub Actions to automatically run tests, build applications, and deploy to staging or production environments.

- **CI/CD Tools**: Use tools like Jenkins, CircleCI, or GitHub Actions to automate testing, building, and deployment as part of the workflow.

3. Define Roles and Permissions

In larger teams, define roles and permissions to ensure that the right people have the right level of access to repositories and branches. For example:

- **Access Control**: Limit who can push directly to `main` or `production` branches.
- **Code Reviews**: Require multiple approvals before merging a pull request into key branches.

4. Regular Communication and Documentation

Ensure that the entire team is on the same page regarding the Git workflow. Use team meetings or internal documentation to explain how the workflow works, how to resolve conflicts, and what tools and processes to follow.

- **Document the Workflow**: Create clear documentation for the Git workflow, including branching strategies, commit message conventions, and how to handle issues like merge conflicts.

5. Training and Onboarding

Provide training to new team members on the Git workflow and how to use the version control system efficiently. This should cover everything from basic Git commands to understanding the team-specific workflow and branch strategies.

Conclusion

In this chapter, we discussed various Git workflows such as **GitHub Flow**, **Git Flow**, **feature branching**, **trunk-based development**, and **GitOps**. Each of these workflows serves different purposes and is suitable for different types of projects and teams. By choosing the right workflow and implementing it effectively, teams can enhance collaboration, streamline development, and reduce issues related to merging and branching. Ultimately, selecting the right Git workflow depends on the project requirements, team size, and release cadence, but having a well-defined and consistent workflow will improve productivity and code quality in any team environment.

CHAPTER 25

ADVANCED GITHUB FEATURES

GitHub provides a wide range of features that can greatly enhance the development workflow, especially for teams that rely on automation, collaboration, and project management. In this chapter, we'll dive into **advanced GitHub features** such as using the **GitHub API** for automating tasks, leveraging **GitHub Actions and Workflows** for DevOps, managing projects with **GitHub Projects and Kanban boards**, and using **GitHub Discussions and Wikis** for documentation and collaboration.

GitHub API for Automating Tasks

The **GitHub API** is a powerful tool that allows you to interact programmatically with GitHub repositories, users, issues, pull requests, and more. This API can be used to automate repetitive tasks, integrate with third-party services, and create custom workflows.

1. What is the GitHub API?

The GitHub API is a RESTful API that allows developers to access and modify various aspects of GitHub, such as repositories, issues, pull requests, and more. It allows for automated interaction with GitHub without the need for manual input through the GitHub web interface.

- **Key Features of the GitHub API**:
  - **Repositories**: Create, update, and manage repositories.
  - **Issues and Pull Requests**: Automate issue creation, manage comments, and track pull requests.
  - **Actions**: Trigger GitHub Actions and workflows programmatically.
  - **Users and Organizations**: Manage users, teams, and organizations.
  - **Webhooks**: Set up webhooks to trigger external services based on events on GitHub.

2. Common Use Cases for the GitHub API

- **Automating Issue Management**: Automatically create or update issues based on certain events, like a new commit or a pull request merge.
- **Managing Pull Requests**: Automatically open, close, or merge pull requests based on specific conditions.
- **Integration with CI/CD Pipelines**: Use the API to trigger builds or deployments from external systems like Jenkins or CircleCI.

- **Custom Dashboards**: Build custom dashboards to visualize GitHub repository data, such as pull request status, commit history, and issue tracking.

3. Example of Using the GitHub API

Here's an example of how you can use the GitHub API to create an issue in a repository using a simple `curl` command:

bash

```
curl -X POST -H "Authorization: token
YOUR_GITHUB_TOKEN" \
    -d '{"title": "Bug in the application",
"body": "Details about the bug..."}' \

https://api.github.com/repos/username/repositor
y/issues
```

This command will create a new issue in the specified GitHub repository.

GitHub Actions and Workflows for DevOps

GitHub Actions is a feature within GitHub that allows you to automate workflows directly in your repositories. GitHub Actions can be used to automate various tasks, including continuous integration (CI), continuous delivery (CD), testing, deployments, and more.

1. What are GitHub Actions?

GitHub Actions are custom workflows that are defined in YAML files and run on GitHub's infrastructure. You can automate tasks like:

- Running tests on every push.
- Deploying to staging or production environments.
- Linting code.
- Running security checks.

2. GitHub Actions Workflows

A **workflow** is defined by a `.yml` file located in the `.github/workflows` directory of a repository. These workflows are made up of multiple jobs, which contain a series of steps.

- **Workflow Example**: Here's an example of a simple GitHub Actions workflow that runs tests on every push to the `main` branch:

```yaml
name: Node.js CI
```

```
on:
  push:
    branches:
      - main

jobs:
  build:
    runs-on: ubuntu-latest

    steps:
      - name: Checkout repository
        uses: actions/checkout@v2

      - name: Set up Node.js
        uses: actions/setup-node@v2
        with:
          node-version: '14'

      - name: Install dependencies
        run: npm install

      - name: Run tests
        run: npm test
```

- **Key Sections of the Workflow**:
  - **on**: Specifies the events that trigger the workflow (e.g., push to the `main` branch).

255

o **jobs**: Defines a set of jobs that run sequentially or in parallel.

o **steps**: Each job consists of a series of steps that can be actions or shell commands.

3. Common Use Cases for GitHub Actions

- **Continuous Integration (CI)**: Automatically run tests and linting on every push or pull request.
- **Continuous Deployment (CD)**: Automatically deploy code to a staging or production environment after successful tests.
- **Automated Releases**: Automate versioning and release creation based on tags or commits.
- **Scheduling**: Run periodic tasks (e.g., nightly builds, security scans) using scheduled events.

4. Managing Secrets in GitHub Actions

GitHub Actions allows you to store sensitive data like API keys, passwords, and other secrets. Secrets are stored in the repository settings and are encrypted at rest.

- **Using Secrets in Actions**:

```yaml
- name: Deploy to Production
```

```
run: |
  echo "Deploying to production..."
env:
  API_KEY: ${{ secrets.API_KEY }}
```

Managing Projects Using GitHub Projects and Kanban Boards

GitHub Projects offers project management features, allowing you to organize and prioritize tasks within your repositories. GitHub Projects uses **Kanban boards**, making it easy to track progress through columns such as **To Do**, **In Progress**, and **Done**.

1. What is GitHub Projects?

GitHub Projects provides a flexible, visual way to manage tasks within a repository. You can create boards to manage issues, pull requests, and notes, and track their progress using columns and cards.

- **Kanban Boards**: GitHub Projects supports Kanban-style boards where tasks (issues, pull requests) are organized into columns based on their current state.
- **Automation**: GitHub Projects allows you to automate workflows like moving cards between columns when the associated issue changes status (e.g., when a pull request is merged, the card automatically moves to the "Done" column).

2. Creating and Managing Projects

To create a new project:

1. Go to the **Projects** tab in your repository or organization.
2. Click **New Project** and choose the template (e.g., Basic Kanban, Automated Kanban).
3. Add columns and cards (issues or pull requests) to organize your work.
4. Use automation to transition tasks based on status changes.

3. Tracking Progress with Kanban Boards

Each column represents a stage in the project's lifecycle (e.g., **To Do**, **In Progress**, **Done**). You can drag and drop cards (issues or pull requests) between columns to track their status.

- **Automating Transitions**: For example, you can set up an automation rule that moves an issue card from **In Progress** to **Done** when the associated pull request is merged.

4. Integrating GitHub Projects with GitHub Actions

GitHub Projects can be integrated with GitHub Actions to automate tasks like moving issues or pull requests to different columns based on status updates (e.g., when an issue is closed, it can be automatically moved to the "Done" column).

Leveraging GitHub Discussions and Wikis for Documentation

GitHub provides tools for team collaboration and documentation through **GitHub Discussions** and **Wikis**. These tools help organize knowledge sharing, troubleshooting, and community interaction within your project.

1. GitHub Discussions

GitHub Discussions is a feature that allows you to engage with your project's community, ask questions, share knowledge, and discuss ideas. It's a great way to keep conversations within GitHub without relying on external tools.

- **Key Features of GitHub Discussions**:
    o **Categories**: Organize discussions by categories (e.g., Q&A, Ideas, Announcements).
    o **Discussions and Replies**: Collaborators can post discussions, reply to others, and pin important discussions.
    o **Integrating with Issues**: Discussions can be linked to GitHub issues and pull requests, making it easier to collaborate on specific topics.

259

- **When to Use GitHub Discussions**:
  - Ideal for project-related discussions, Q&A, and community engagement.
  - Useful for technical support or brainstorming new ideas without cluttering the issue tracker.

2. GitHub Wikis

GitHub Wikis are dedicated spaces within repositories where you can store and manage documentation. Unlike Discussions, Wikis are focused on long-form documentation such as tutorials, architecture diagrams, setup guides, and API references.

- **Key Features of GitHub Wikis**:
  - **Markdown Support**: Wikis use Markdown, making it easy to write and format documentation.
  - **Multiple Pages**: You can create a multi-page documentation system with links between pages.
  - **Version Control**: Since Wikis are part of Git repositories, all changes to the Wiki are versioned, making it easy to track changes over time.
- **When to Use GitHub Wikis**:
  - Ideal for maintaining project documentation, such as user guides, installation instructions, and API references.

o   Useful for keeping project-related information centralized and easy to access.

Conclusion

In this chapter, we explored advanced GitHub features that enhance collaboration, automation, and project management. The **GitHub API** allows you to automate tasks and integrate GitHub with external services. **GitHub Actions** and **Workflows** provide powerful tools for automating DevOps processes, including CI/CD. **GitHub Projects and Kanban boards** help teams organize and manage tasks effectively, while **GitHub Discussions** and **Wikis** enable collaborative knowledge sharing and detailed documentation. By leveraging these advanced features, teams can streamline workflows, enhance productivity, and improve the overall development process on GitHub.

CHAPTER 26

GIT AND GITHUB IN THE REAL WORLD

Git and GitHub are not just tools used by individual developers; they are central to the workflows of some of the world's largest companies, open-source projects, and even personal projects. In this chapter, we will explore **real-world case studies** of how companies and projects use Git and GitHub, delve into **GitHub's role in popular open-source projects**, examine **how large organizations leverage Git for distributed teams**, and discuss **how Git and GitHub can be used for personal projects** such as portfolios, blogs, and websites.

Case Studies: How Companies and Projects Use Git and GitHub

Git and GitHub have become essential tools in modern software development, widely used in a range of industries from startups to large enterprises. Below are some real-world case studies that highlight how different companies and projects use Git and GitHub.

1. Microsoft: Embracing Open Source with GitHub

Microsoft's acquisition of GitHub in 2018 marked a significant shift in the company's approach to open-source development. Before this acquisition, Microsoft had been largely known for its closed-source software. However, with GitHub, Microsoft now heavily relies on Git and GitHub for both open-source and proprietary development.

- **How Microsoft Uses GitHub**:
    - **GitHub for Open Source**: Microsoft has become one of the largest contributors to open-source projects, hosting popular projects such as **VS Code, PowerShell**, and **.NET Core** on GitHub.
    - **Internal Collaboration**: Microsoft uses GitHub internally to support distributed teams working on both open-source and closed-source projects. Teams work together using GitHub's features like issues, pull requests, and Actions for continuous integration and deployment.
    - **GitHub Actions for CI/CD**: Microsoft's projects like **VS Code** leverage GitHub Actions to automate testing, building, and deployment workflows.

2. Google: Distributed Development with Git

Google has a large number of internal projects and open-source contributions, and it uses Git for both individual and team-based projects. While Google has its internal version control system called **Piper**, it also uses Git for open-source projects and distributed development.

- **How Google Uses Git**:
  - o **Open-Source Projects**: Projects like **Kubernetes**, **Go**, and **TensorFlow** are developed on GitHub, where Google has vast communities of developers contributing.
  - o **Internal Use**: Google uses Git for distributed teams and version control of various projects. It leverages tools like **Google Cloud Build** for CI/CD workflows.
  - o **Collaboration and Review**: Google's open-source projects on GitHub rely on Git's pull request model to review code and ensure that contributions meet the necessary standards before being merged.

3. GitHub's Role in Startups

Startups and smaller tech companies benefit from GitHub's flexible workflows and collaborative tools. Many startups use

GitHub to store their codebase, track issues, and manage their development process from day one.

- **How Startups Use GitHub**:
  - o **Collaboration and Version Control**: Startups use GitHub's collaborative features to allow developers to work on different parts of the codebase at the same time. With GitHub's pull request system, code reviews and discussions are streamlined.
  - o **Project Management**: GitHub Projects, Kanban boards, and issue tracking help startups organize tasks and plan releases efficiently.
  - o **Integration with CI/CD**: Startups rely on GitHub Actions or third-party CI/CD services to automate testing, building, and deployment, ensuring fast and continuous delivery of features and updates.

GitHub in Popular Open-Source Projects

GitHub has become the platform of choice for open-source development. Many of the most popular open-source projects are hosted on GitHub, where developers around the world can collaborate, contribute, and maintain projects.

1. Linux Kernel

The **Linux Kernel**, one of the most significant open-source projects in the world, uses Git for version control. Though it initially used other systems, the Linux kernel switched to Git early on, mainly because of its speed and flexibility.

- **How the Linux Kernel Uses Git**:
    - o **Distributed Development**: The Linux Kernel has thousands of contributors around the world, working on different aspects of the kernel. Git's distributed model makes it easy for contributors to work independently and merge their changes into the main project.
    - o **Submodules**: Git's support for submodules allows the kernel to manage dependencies and external modules efficiently.
    - o **Branching and Merging**: The project's large codebase and frequent updates require a well-structured workflow, with branches dedicated to bug fixes, features, and version releases.

2. React

React, the JavaScript library for building user interfaces, is another highly successful open-source project hosted on GitHub.

Managed by Facebook, React has a large community of contributors and a robust GitHub presence.

- **How React Uses GitHub**:
  - **Issue Tracking and Pull Requests**: React uses GitHub Issues to track bugs and new feature requests. Contributions are submitted via pull requests, and the community participates in code reviews.
  - **Documentation and Discussions**: React's documentation is maintained on GitHub, where users can contribute updates. The React team also uses GitHub Discussions to engage with the community and gather feedback.
  - **GitHub Actions for CI/CD**: React uses GitHub Actions to run automated tests and build processes whenever new code is pushed.

3. Kubernetes

Kubernetes, a container orchestration platform, is a widely used open-source project for managing and automating the deployment, scaling, and management of containerized applications. It is hosted on GitHub and relies on Git for version control.

- **How Kubernetes Uses GitHub**:

- o **Collaborative Development**: Kubernetes has thousands of contributors, and GitHub's branching and pull request model is essential for managing contributions.
- o **CI/CD and Automation**: Kubernetes uses GitHub Actions and other CI/CD tools to automate testing, building, and deployment, ensuring that changes to the project are verified before merging into the main branch.

How Large Organizations Leverage Git for Distributed Teams

In large organizations, Git is an essential tool for managing distributed teams, allowing for efficient collaboration and seamless integration of changes from multiple developers working in different time zones or locations.

1. Collaboration Across Distributed Teams

- **Version Control**: Git's distributed nature ensures that every team member has a complete of the repository, which means they can work offline and push changes when convenient.
- **Pull Requests and Code Review**: Teams use GitHub's pull request system to review changes before merging

them into the main codebase, ensuring that code quality is maintained across remote teams.

- **Issue Tracking**: GitHub's issue tracker is used to report bugs, suggest features, and assign tasks to developers across teams, ensuring everyone stays aligned on goals.

2. Continuous Integration and Deployment (CI/CD)

Large organizations often use GitHub Actions or third-party CI/CD tools to automate their deployment processes. By integrating Git with CI/CD pipelines, companies can:

- Automatically run tests on every push.
- Deploy code to different environments (e.g., staging, production) when changes are merged into specific branches.
- Monitor the status of builds and deployments directly from GitHub.

3. Security and Access Control

GitHub's robust **access control** features allow large organizations to manage team permissions effectively. Administrators can restrict access to sensitive code, manage collaborators, and ensure that only authorized personnel can make changes to critical parts of the project.

Git and GitHub for Personal Projects: Portfolios, Blogs, and Websites

Git and GitHub are not just for team projects; they are also excellent tools for managing **personal projects**, including portfolios, blogs, and websites. GitHub provides a centralized location to store and showcase your work while also enabling version control for your personal projects.

1. Personal Portfolios

Many developers use GitHub to host their **portfolio websites**. By creating a repository for your portfolio and using GitHub Pages, you can deploy your portfolio directly from GitHub. GitHub Pages is a free hosting service that allows you to publish static websites directly from your repository.

- **How to Host a Portfolio on GitHub**:
    1. Create a repository with the name `username.github.io`.
    2. Push your HTML, CSS, and JavaScript files to the repository.
    3. Enable GitHub Pages in the repository settings, and your portfolio will be live at `https://username.github.io`.

2. Personal Blogs

GitHub is also an excellent platform for hosting **blogs**, especially static blogs built using static site generators like **Jekyll** or **Hugo**. GitHub Pages supports Jekyll natively, making it easy to publish blog posts with markdown files.

- **How to Set Up a Blog on GitHub**:
  1. Create a repository for your blog.
  2. Use Jekyll or another static site generator to create the blog structure.
  3. Push your blog content to the repository and enable GitHub Pages to host the blog.

3. Personal Websites

GitHub also makes it easy to manage personal websites using the same workflow as for portfolios and blogs. You can track changes to your website's code, manage content, and collaborate with others if needed.

Conclusion

In this chapter, we explored how **Git and GitHub** are used in the real world, from **large organizations** and **popular open-source projects** to **personal projects** like portfolios, blogs, and websites. GitHub has become an essential tool for teams, companies, and developers worldwide, facilitating **collaboration**, **version control**, and **automation** through features like **GitHub Actions** and **GitHub Pages**. Whether you're working on enterprise-level applications, contributing to open-source, or managing personal projects, Git and GitHub are powerful tools that support a wide variety of workflows and use cases.

CHAPTER 27

THE FUTURE OF GIT AND GITHUB

As technology continues to evolve, so do the tools and systems we rely on to build and manage software. Git and GitHub have revolutionized the way developers collaborate and version control their code. However, both Git and GitHub are continuously evolving to meet the growing demands of modern software development. In this chapter, we'll explore the **upcoming features in Git and GitHub**, **the future of version control**, **alternatives to Git**, and the **evolving trends in software development**. We'll also provide guidance on **continuous learning** and **resources to stay up-to-date**.

Upcoming Features in Git and GitHub

1. Upcoming Git Features

Git is an open-source project that evolves through contributions from developers worldwide. While Git's core functionality has been stable for years, the community continues to improve its performance, user experience, and compatibility with modern workflows.

- **Performance Improvements**: One of the major areas of focus for the Git community is improving performance, especially for large repositories. There are ongoing efforts to make operations like cloning, fetching, and pulling faster for repositories with millions of files or large histories.

- **Better Merge Conflict Resolution**: Git's current conflict resolution process can be cumbersome, and there are efforts to improve how conflicts are detected and handled. Future Git releases may include more intelligent conflict resolution tools, perhaps with better visualization and automatic suggestions.

- **Improved Rebase Features**: Git's `rebase` command is widely used for cleaning up commit histories. Developers are working on making `rebase` more user-friendly, especially for beginners, by offering clearer instructions and better error messages.

- **Multi-Repository Support**: Git is evolving to handle multiple repositories and submodules more efficiently, which is particularly important as microservices and distributed architectures become more common. This may include more robust support for managing dependencies and interactions across multiple repositories.

2. Upcoming GitHub Features

GitHub continuously improves its features to support more advanced workflows, enhance collaboration, and facilitate seamless integration with other tools and services. Here are some anticipated updates:

- **GitHub Copilot Integration**: GitHub's AI-powered code completion tool, **GitHub Copilot**, is continually being enhanced. We can expect deeper integration with GitHub repositories, offering suggestions for code completion, documentation, and even unit tests directly within the GitHub interface.

- **Improved Project Management Tools**: GitHub is working on improving the project management features with more advanced Kanban board functionalities, better automation for task tracking, and enhanced visibility into project progress.

- **Advanced Security Features**: GitHub has already introduced features like **Dependabot** for automatic security updates, but we can expect even more advanced security capabilities, such as better integration with vulnerability scanning tools, enhanced access controls, and improved management of secrets.

- **GitHub Actions Enhancements**: GitHub Actions, the tool for automating workflows, is one of GitHub's most powerful features. In the future, we may see more advanced integrations with third-party services, faster execution times, and easier-to-use workflows for non-technical users.

- **Better Collaboration Tools**: GitHub is continuously enhancing collaboration features like **GitHub Discussions** and **GitHub Wikis**. We can expect improvements in these areas to support richer community interactions, better documentation, and smoother code review processes.

What the Future Holds for Version Control

1. Git's Dominance

Despite the rise of other version control systems, Git is expected to remain the dominant version control system for the foreseeable future. Its distributed nature, speed, flexibility, and widespread adoption make it the preferred tool for software development.

- **Better Support for Large Teams**: Git is evolving to handle more complex workflows, making it easier for large teams with multiple sub-teams and departments to collaborate on large codebases.
- **Focus on Automation and Integration**: As software development becomes more automated, Git will continue to integrate with tools like **CI/CD** systems,

containerization tools (e.g., Docker), and **cloud platforms** to streamline the development process.

2. The Emergence of AI and Automation

The integration of **artificial intelligence (AI)** and **machine learning (ML)** into version control systems is an exciting trend. Git and GitHub will likely become more intelligent by integrating AI-driven tools for:

- **Code review**: AI could assist in reviewing code, suggesting improvements, and automatically detecting bugs or potential vulnerabilities.
- **Conflict Resolution**: AI could be used to detect potential merge conflicts earlier and offer smarter conflict resolution strategies.
- **Automated Testing and Deployment**: AI-powered tools can help test and deploy code faster and more efficiently.

3. Cloud-Native Version Control

As cloud-native development and microservices become the norm, version control systems like Git will increasingly integrate with cloud services. GitHub's cloud-first approach with **GitHub Actions** and **GitHub Pages** is a step in this direction, and we can expect more features that enable developers to manage code across multiple cloud environments seamlessly.

Alternatives to Git and Evolving Trends in Software Development

While Git has become the standard version control system, there are still alternatives that are suited to different use cases. Let's explore some of these alternatives and how they fit into the evolving landscape of version control.

1. SVN (Subversion)

SVN remains a popular centralized version control system, particularly in legacy projects or for teams that prefer a simpler workflow. However, it lacks the flexibility and power of Git for managing distributed teams and large codebases.

- **When to Use SVN**: SVN is still a viable option for small teams or projects that do not require extensive branching and merging. It's also preferred in some industries that require strict control over versioned files and code.

2. Mercurial

Mercurial is a distributed version control system that's similar to Git but with a simpler interface and fewer advanced features. While Git has largely overtaken Mercurial in popularity, Mercurial is still used by some companies, especially those who value simplicity over advanced branching and merging.

- **When to Use Mercurial**: Mercurial is suitable for teams that want the benefits of distributed version control without the complexity of Git. It's also a good choice for smaller teams or projects that don't need the extensive features of Git.

3. Perforce (Helix Core)

Perforce is another alternative that is often used for large codebases, especially in industries like gaming or digital media. Perforce uses a centralized model but offers high performance for handling large files and repositories.

- **When to Use Perforce**: Perforce is ideal for industries where large binary files are frequently versioned, such as video games, where handling massive assets is essential.

4. GitOps

GitOps is an evolving trend that combines Git with operations automation. GitOps allows for continuous deployment and operations using Git as the source of truth for infrastructure configurations, enabling declarative infrastructure management.

- **When to Use GitOps**: GitOps is ideal for teams managing cloud infrastructure and services. It ensures that infrastructure is versioned, auditable, and automatically updated based on changes to Git repositories.

Continuous Learning: Resources to Stay Up-to-Date

The world of version control and software development is constantly evolving. To stay ahead, it's essential to keep learning and stay up-to-date with new features, trends, and best practices.

1. Git and GitHub Documentation

- **Git Documentation**: The official Git documentation is an excellent resource for understanding Git's inner workings and keeping up with new releases.
- **GitHub Docs**: GitHub's documentation covers everything from basic usage to advanced features like Actions, GitHub Pages, and security.

2. Online Courses and Tutorials

- **Codecademy**: Codecademy offers interactive tutorials on Git and GitHub for beginners and advanced users.
- **Udemy**: Udemy has a variety of courses on Git, GitHub, and GitOps, offering deep dives into version control concepts.
- **LinkedIn Learning**: LinkedIn Learning provides comprehensive tutorials on using Git and GitHub for development and DevOps.

3. Developer Blogs and Communities

- **GitHub Blog**: The GitHub Blog is a great resource for staying updated on new features, tutorials, and best practices.
- **Stack Overflow**: Engage with the developer community on Stack Overflow to find answers to common issues and keep up with new Git and GitHub tips.
- **Reddit**: Subreddits like r/git and r/github are great for discussing the latest trends and sharing knowledge with fellow developers.

4. Books and Publications

- **Pro Git**: **"Pro Git"** is an excellent, free book on Git available at progit.org, which covers Git from basics to advanced features.
- **GitHub for Developers**: There are many books on GitHub and GitOps, like **"GitHub for Developers"** and **"GitOps: Continuous Deployment and Infrastructure Automation with Git"** that provide in-depth knowledge.

Conclusion

In this chapter, we explored the **future of Git and GitHub**, including upcoming features, new trends in version control, and the continued importance of Git in the development landscape. As Git and GitHub evolve, developers can expect more powerful features for automation, collaboration, and security. We also discussed **alternatives to Git**, such as **SVN**, **Mercurial**, and **Perforce**, and how they fit into the evolving trends in software development. Finally, we highlighted resources for **continuous learning**, ensuring that you can stay up-to-date with the latest developments in version control and GitHub. The future of version control looks bright, and staying current with the tools will help you maintain an efficient, collaborative, and modern development workflow.

www.ingramcontent.com/pod-product-compliance
Lightning Source LLC
La Vergne TN
LVHW022337060326
832902LV00022B/4090